THE EXECUTIVE AT WORK

THE EXECUTIVE AT WORK

Melvin T. Copeland

Director of Research and George Baker Professor of Administration, Graduate School of Business Administration, Harvard University

HARVARD UNIVERSITY PRESS
Cambridge, Massachusetts
1951

Distributed in Great Britain by
Geoffrey Cumberlege
Oxford University Press
London

Printed in the United States of America

CONTENTS

THE EXECUTIVE AT WORK

I

The Authority of the Executive

The purpose of this book is to discuss the elements of executive achievement. It deals primarily with executive leadership in corporate business enterprises, but most of the conclusions, with some fairly apparent modifications, also hold good for businesses conducted by individual proprietorships or partnerships. Many of the conclusions, furthermore, apply to executive achievement in nonbusiness enterprises, such as educational institutions and various social and political organizations. The problems of administration in many other kinds of enterprises are much the same as in business corporations.

Administration is one of the most prevalent types of responsibility, yet, like the air we breathe, it commonly is taken for granted and often not comprehended. Two examples may help to illustrate this noncomprehension.

In the course of a long chat recently with a social worker, I discovered that to him business administration connoted chiefly greed and avarice. He was a college graduate who had served as a university instructor in English before becoming a social worker. He was thoroughly honest and sincere in his opinions. His views, to be sure, were not logically crystallized. They were, in fact, somewhat incoherent, but he obviously had deep feelings on the subject.

When reference was made to training men for executive work, his remarks indicated that he failed to see why anyone who is at all public spirited should want to increase the supply of those rascals. Why stimulate more avarice and greed? He apparently felt that there are plenty of men who can run small businesses; consequently, why should there be any lack of men for managerial positions? Implicit in that attitude was the assumption that the chief difference between running a small business and a larger enterprise is the ability to exploit others and get a big salary to the disadvantage of the other employees. To him, the size of the economic pie was fixed, and the more that was paid for executive salaries, the less was left for the men who did the real work. He was heartily in favor of having executive salaries limited to a maximum of $25,000, to him an astronomical figure.

These views came out in the course of a casual discussion. They were not expressed in just the terms that I have used, and they appeared in numerous different forms. The gist of his views was that administration is the knack of exploiting others.

I judge that there are many other persons who feel the same way. A carpenter, for instance, remarked to me with a shrug during the worst of the December campaign in Korea that the Korean war, after all, was probably brought on by some big company trying to get control of a new oil field.

I am reporting these observations without any intent at criticism. They constitute, I believe, some very important facts — because such attitudes are facts whether or not the attitudes are correct.

Not long before I had this conversation with the social worker, the chief executive of a large business corporation was in my office discussing a variety of business problems with a group of my associates. During the course of our talk, I had occasion to remark that I had read a considerable number of biographies and autobiographies of distinguished American business executives and that in those works there was almost no reference to administration, the job of organizing an enterprise and getting results accomplished through people. A few days later I learned that our guest also had written an autobiography, a fact of which I previously had not been aware. It is a very interesting book, but out of 230 pages there are only about three pages on which there is any reference to administration. He had not told the story of his own great contribution in building an enterprise.

If the business executives who have been conspicuously successful in administration are not sufficiently conscious of those achievements to present them clearly and forcefully, how can we expect the social worker and the carpenter to have a better concept of administration?

Since so few executives are articulate on the subject with which they are most familiar, I have had to fall back largely on my own observations and experience in undertaking to make an analysis of what is involved in effective administration. This background, perhaps I should add, covers a period of forty-odd years and includes not only the analysis and discussion of hundreds of concrete problems of business administration in the classroom but also supervision of business research activities, service as an adviser to the executives of various companies, participation in university and college administrative work, membership in several governmental organizations, and innumerable visits from executives concerned with all sorts of problems. Such is the fund of experience upon which I have drawn. In the chapters that follow, furthermore, I have made frequent references to research reports published by my associates while I have been Director of Research at the Harvard Business School, since in a sense they also constitute part of my own experience.

To me an active business enterprise is rife with vibrancies

and vibrant personalities. Consequently a second reason for drawing so extensively on my own observations and experience is to attempt thereby to reflect some of the vibrancies which I myself have felt. During the last fifty years numerous books and articles have been published on the theory and practices of business organization and management. I have some acquaintance with that literature, and I intend to imply no disparagement by not reviewing it more extensively here. I merely have been pursuing a somewhat different objective.

As a first step in analyzing the vibrant activities of an executive, I propose to discuss the authority of an executive.

The source of authority

For all but the smallest undertakings, a business enterprise consists of a group of people organized to carry on the operations for a profit. A boatbuilder, working alone in a little shop, does everything himself, but as soon as he hires someone to work with him, he has to assign tasks, give instructions, and check on results. In other words, he has to be at least a part-time manager. In a large shipbuilding company, the operating group includes not only many laborers of a variety of skills, but also engineers, draftsmen, inspectors, accountants, salesmen, clerical workers, and various other categories of employees, with a hierarchy of foremen, superintendents, managers, and executives. A division of labor takes place not only in the shop but also through the managerial organization. At the head of that organization stands an executive, a commander-in-chief, as it were, who focuses the managerial tasks. With variations in details an analogous situation exists in other modern business enterprises.

In a business corporation the responsibility for the management of operations is delegated to the chief executive by the board of directors.

That delegation of responsibility, however, does not automatically vest the executive with authority. Real authority is not a power attained by the bestowal of a title, by an entry on an organization chart, by the issuance of a directive, or by a laying on of hands. Real authority must be won by the action of the executive himself. His appointment to office merely gives him an opportunity to demonstrate his qualities of leadership, to win the esteem, respect, and support of the members of the organization with whom he is to work. It is thereby that he gains authority.

The following situation is a particularly common one. The chief executive of an industrial company, under whose guidance and leadership the company had grown and prospered for many years, retired to the chairmanship of the board of directors. A promising junior executive from within the company was promoted to the presidency. Since the chairman continued to spend several hours each day in the office, the heads of the operating departments, who had been selected and trained by him, continued to go to him frequently for advice and instructions, thus by-passing the new president. Titles had been changed, but procedures remained largely unaltered. The new president was in a difficult position. He wished to retain for the benefit of the corporation the wisdom and counsel of his predecessor. He also realized that an abrupt attempt to shatter old loyalties or an outright insistence on a radical change in procedures not only might embarrass the chairman, to whom the company owed real gratitude; such a procedure also probably would arouse widespread antagonism toward him and resentment among his associates in the administrative organization. In this instance the new president chose to follow a slower but less antagonizing program, and as one step set up a new budget committee to consider requests for departmental appropriations and to report thereon to him before they were presented to the board of directors. Gradually he introduced a change in habits and began to secure recognition of his executive position.

In contrast to the foregoing experience, when Mr. Conant was elected to the presidency of Harvard University to succeed Mr. Lowell, Mr. Lowell betook himself to Boston to live and scrupulously avoided any participation in the administrative affairs of the university. Mr. Conant still had real problems to face in securing acceptance of his leadership in some quarters of the university, but his task was simplified by the wise course which Mr. Lowell pursued.

Another type of situation is exemplified by the case of a large manufacturing company in which a new president inherited a bag full of company politics. The first president of the company, which had been formed by the merger of several corporations, was a forceful promoter. During his regime the company had expanded substantially in size. In the later years of his incumbency over forty plants were being operated by the company. A central sales office was maintained in New York City, but each plant operated with a high degree of autonomy. Each plant had its own designing department and was permitted, if it chose, to copy designs manufactured at other plants and to engage in price competition with other plants of the company. One result was that competition between company units sometimes was keener than competition with other manufacturers. Another concomitant result was to make the company rife with internal rivalries and politics.

After the first president retired, the board of directors elected as his successor a man with a notable record for proficiency in merchandising, but the choice was not a happy one. To be sure, the company needed better merchandise management. But it needed far more urgently an executive leader who could rescue an organization undergoing social disintegration. The new president proceeded to take over a few functions from the plants into the central office, but the net result was to intensify the resentment and disaffection in the ranks. He never succeeded in surmounting the political difficulties which he inherited, and after a few years he resigned. He had the title of chief executive, but he did not achieve executive leadership.

A classic example of a test of leadership occurred when Charles W. Eliot became president of Harvard University. Up to that time the Medical School as well as the Law School had been administered rather loosely. Mr. Eliot proposed to tighten up the administration and improve instruction. One of the leading members of the Medical School faculty was Dr. Oliver Wendell Holmes. In April 1870, six months after Mr. Eliot's inauguration, Dr. Holmes summed up the situation as follows:

Mr. Eliot makes the Corporation meet *twice* a month instead of once. He comes to the meeting of every Faculty, ours among the rest, and keeps us up to eleven and twelve o'clock at night discussing new arrangements . . .

"How is it? I should like to ask," said one of our number the other evening, "that this Faculty has gone on for eighty years, managing its own affairs and doing it well — for the Medical School is the most flourishing department connected with the college — how is it that we have been going on so well in the same orderly path for eighty years, and now within *three or four months* it is proposed to change all our modes of carrying on the school — it seems very extraordinary, and I should like to know how it happens."

"I can answer Dr. ——'s question very easily," said the bland, grave young man: "There is a new President."

The tranquil assurance of this answer had an effect such as I hardly ever knew produced by the most eloquent sentences I ever heard uttered.[1]

[1] Henry James, *Charles William Eliot* (Boston: Houghton Mifflin, 1930), I, 283–284.

Testing an executive

It seems to be a quite universal trait of human nature for at least some members of a group to put to a test any new person "of authority." In the classroom, students try out a new teacher to find out how far they can go, and many a teacher has been broken by a failure to pass that first test. In a military or naval unit, the men try out a new officer. The same sort of thing occurs on professional athletic teams. The following statement is quoted from Bob Dunbar's column in the *Boston Herald,* December 31, 1941:

> The more we hear and read about the ideas of baseball men, the more we realize that a vast majority of them are pulling for Mel Ott to make good as manager of the Giants . . . It is a fact, however, that the great guys of baseball do not always click as managers and this may be true of Ottie, who has yet to demonstrate that he has the intestinal fortitude to say "yes" or "no" when necessary, even when it hurts the feelings of a veteran and established player . . . Big League managers not only need to know the game, but they must know the players, must command their respect and retain that respect, regardless of how tough the going. And any man who can't say a strong unqualified "no" when necessary simply is wasting his time taking up a managerial portfolio in any company.

Another example of the challenging of a new executive in the business field illustrates an experience which in substance is continually being duplicated in many other companies. In this particular instance, the company was one of medium size. It had been owned and managed by members of the same family for several generations. In 1935 the president of the company died. His brother was elected president, but he was only nominally active, and the chief executive job was delegated to a man, not a member of the family, who was promoted from the sales managership to be general manager of the company. Shortly after the new general manager was appointed, the factory manager requested the general manager to give him a raise in salary and threatened to leave for another job if his request was not granted. The factory manager knew perfectly well that the company's financial condition was not such as to permit the granting of the increase in salary at that time, and his threat of resigning was an emotional manifestation. He was envious of the new general manager, not so much because of any desire to have the position himself as because of the changed relationships of the two men in the social hierarchy of the company. The factory manager was reluctant emotionally to face the fact that his former peer was now his boss. The general manager refused the request, with an explanation of his reasons, and the factory manager did not resign. The new general manager thereby passed a critical test.

Such jealous reactions as those just cited are likely to occur whenever a promotion is made from within the ranks. If an outsider is hired to fill such a position, furthermore, he also usually encounters emotional opposition, stemming from other causes. Such experiences as these occur in every organization — business, political, educational, and social.

My own personal experience with such challenges has been on a modest scale. I have been tried out by scores of classes of students, of course, a few of those tests being amusing, but most of them quite incidental, and none fatal. Undergoing those classroom tests became commonplace early in my teaching life. In some of my ventures into the outside world, I also have encountered similar challenges. One of these, for instance, was in connection with the Massachusetts Committee on Post-War Readjustment, appointed by Governor Saltonstall in November 1941. There were thirty–three members on the committee, representing a wide variety of interests, and the Governor asked me to serve as chairman. The Governor bestowed the title, but the real authority of the chairman was put to a test at least four times within the first six months of the committee's existence.

The first of these tests came at the second meeting of the committee. A few minutes before the meeting was to be called to order, one of the members, a retired business executive who had played a prominent part in civilian defense activities in the First World War, came to me quietly to proffer his administrative help. He told me that he knew how busy I was and that he would be glad to help me out. He then offered to act as executive director of the committee. I thanked him graciously but assured him that at that time I saw no need for having an executive director appointed. When the meeting got under way, I soon discovered that my would-be helper was attempting to run the meeting from the floor, and presently some polite strong-arm methods had to be utilized to enable the chairman to exercise the real prerogatives of the position in which his appointment nominally had placed him. I had not sought the position. I would have had few regrets at being replaced. But I could not abdicate in favor of a volunteer who primarily wished for more limelight in which to bask — at least I could not abdicate without first consulting the Governor, and in fact I never did bother to tell him about the occurrence.

That episode, as so often happens in such situations, arose quite unexpectedly, without forewarning of any sort. And the other members of the committee, who knew nothing of the preliminary offer of the would-be executive director, had no inkling of what was being attempted on the floor.

Examples of such tests are legion, in organized undertakings of every scale. The reasons why new executives are subjected to such tests are varied. In some instances the tests are prompted by the disappointment of one or more persons in not themselves gaining the limelight. Closely allied to that cause are feelings of envy. In other instances the tests are precipitated by complacent aversion to change or apprehension that old routines may be disrupted. Basically, however, I believe that these tests represent an instinctive and therefore more or less unconscious effort on the part of prospective members of a team to find out whether the person nominally placed in authority has the makings of a leader. Unless a man can pass such an initial test he is not likely to possess the spontaneity, the versatility, the resourcefulness, and the intestinal stamina to meet the crises through which his team must be led. These tests of a new executive may be analogous, in a civilized form, to the physical ordeals by which the chieftains of savage tribes once established their rights to their titles.

An executive sometimes also may find that his authority is being threatened, perhaps inadvertently, by the very source from which he derives his title. The board of directors of a corporation has the responsibility for selecting its chief operating executive and for laying down policies for his guidance.[2] The chief executive properly may expect to receive counsel and support from the board of directors. If he does not receive wholehearted support from the board, he may be unable to maintain leadership even though he continues to hold the title of president.

An example of that sort of situation occurred in the case of a medium-size company when the directors, in 1938, hired a consulting firm to look into the company's organization and operations. The company's sales and those of the industry had been declining for some years. Shortly after the investigation began, the head of the consulting firm proceeded to fire the sales manager and several other department heads and to browbeat others who were not fired. The result was

[2] This matter is discussed at some length in Melvin T. Copeland and Andrew R. Towl, *The Board of Directors and Business Management* (Boston: Division of Research, Harvard Business School, 1947).

to make everyone feel insecure and to break down morale. The consultant was hired by the board of directors and he usurped administrative power. Although the president retained his title, his authority was seriously undermined.

After the consulting firm withdrew, rumors were prevalent in the company that the executive committee of the board of directors was managing operations. Conditions became so serious that the president called a meeting to inform the other executives and staff that nothing was to be done without his personal approval, seeking thereby to reassert an authority which he had lost. It already was too late, however, for the president to correct the situation. When he acquiesced in the assumption of executive prerogatives by the consultant, the president permitted his authority to be compromised. He lost his leadership. Once leadership has been lost, it is extremely difficult to regain the confidence which is essential to its reëstablishment. In this case the executive permitted his authority to be broken from above even though he retained his title.

Acceptance of leadership

The opportunity to exercise leadership is granted by those who choose an executive, but leadership does not become effective until it is accepted by all who participate in the enterprise. Nevertheless, the executive himself has to play a positive part in securing acceptance of his authority. The well-known president of a middle-western university was complaining a few years since that his trustees and faculty were not giving him enough authority to carry out his proposed program. He had not learned that authority has to be won rather than to be received as a bestowal. He had not yet discovered that when a man is given an executive title, the substance of his power comes from his own performance, from his demonstrated ability to have himself *accepted* as the leader of the enterprise.

An executive has a prerogative to issue orders, but those orders do not actually become effective until the executive secures their acceptance by those to whom they are addressed. This point is illustrated by the following experience.[3] In 1941 the chief executive of a large corporation decided that a change in purchasing policy was called for. The company operated over twenty plants located strategically in different industrial areas. Each plant was somewhat specialized in production and its management enjoyed a high degree of autonomy in purchasing materials.

As a result of the decision to change the purchasing policy, an experienced purchasing executive was hired, and the board of directors elected him a vice president with jurisdiction over all purchasing and with discretion to organize the job as he deemed best in the light of the wartime conditions then developing. Shortly thereafter the new vice president made a recommendation to the president, who in turn submitted to the board of directors a resolution requiring each individual plant manager to clear with the head office every purchase contract in excess of $12,000. The board of directors promptly approved the resolution, and the vice president sent a directive to each plant manager notifying him of the new rule. His letters were courteously acknowledged, the plant managers typically assuring the vice president that he could count on their coöperation, but nothing else happened. The plant executives were very busy with defense orders and continued to handle purchasing as in the past. The vice president exercised his prerogative but accomplished nothing.

The vice president in the foregoing case might have bene-

[3] John D. Glover and Ralph M. Hower, *The Administrator* (Chicago: Richard D. Irwin, 1949), pp. 653–654.

fited from the example of an executive of one of the largest corporations in America. This executive, who now is chairman of the board of directors of the company, served as its president for a period of twenty-five years, and it was under his leadership that the company was put on its feet and developed into a highly successful enterprise. In discussing various aspects of business administration recently, he stated very emphatically: "In my 25 years as president of the corporation, I never issued an order. Every important proposal was discussed with the members of my administrative organization, and unless there was general agreement among them as to the acceptability of the proposal, no action was taken." In other words, he secured acceptance of a new move in advance of any final decision. He thus could be assured of support in carrying it out.

The fact that real authority exists only when leadership is accepted by the other participants in the enterprise has other implications. For example, the president of a growing company recently was discussing the advisability of establishing a public market for the stock of the company. He owned forty per cent of the stock, which he had inherited from his father. Although he recognized that the prosperity and growth of the company meant that it was nearing the point when it no longer could be operated most advantageously as a closely held concern, he was apprehensive that he would lose control. As a practical matter, however, his "control" was of secondary importance from a managerial standpoint. Despite his stock ownership, he could continue as the chief executive only if by his own performance he retained the loyalty and support of the officers, employees, creditors, and customers of the company so that it could operate profitably. That loyalty and support could be retained only by leadership, not merely by voting "control" of the stock of the company. In most organizations, power is gained by leadership rather than by control of voting rights.

Let us turn now to certain other aspects of the authority of the executive.

The making of decisions

Administration essentially is a decision-making process, and authority, in a sense, is responsibility for making decisions and for ascertaining that the decisions made are carried out. In business, whether the enterprise be large or small, changes in conditions occur; shifts in personnel take place; conflicts of interest appear; mistakes are made which have to be corrected; and unforeseen contingencies arise. All such developments necessitate the making of decisions. Moreover, just to get the wheels started and to keep them turning, decisions must be made. Someone must decide what is to be done, when, and by whom. For each decision action must be taken, and the primary responsibility for making sure that action is taken rests on whoever makes the decision. Action is induced, however, not by the exercise of physical force, not by the threat of corporal punishment, not even by a threat of any kind except under extreme circumstances. Action is induced rather by leadership.

In a well-managed corporation a framework of policies is set up by the board of directors. But those policies are translated into action by the operating organization. To operate effectively, that organization must have a head, a leader who guides the decisions so as to secure vigorous, concerted, and harmonious action.

Administration, furthermore, is a network of decisions. Each decision which is made has a relationship to other decisions which have preceded and will have a bearing on decisions to be made in the future.

Take for example the decision by the executives of a textile mill to manufacture 100,000 blankets. Let us assume that the company has a plant equipped to manufacture blankets; an operating organization; a working force; a financial and cost accounting system; and at least enough working capital to be solvent. Those assumptions presuppose numerous decisions made in the past. But under those assumptions the decision to manufacture 100,000 blankets is merely the prelude to a long list of other decisions, such as: What is to be the size, weight, and texture of the blankets? What styles and patterns are to be manufactured? In what quantities?

What materials are to be used? When are materials to be purchased? From whom? At what price? What funds are to be used therefor? When are materials to be shipped?

When is production to be started and how is it to be scheduled? Which looms are to be utilized? How many workers are to be employed? How are the blankets to be inspected? How are they to be packed? Are they to be stored? If so, where?

What is to be the selling price? What discounts and credit terms are to be offered to customers? When are orders to be sought? From whom? Are the blankets to be branded or trade-marked? Are they to be advertised? If so, how much is to be spent in advertising? In what media? When?

When are shipments to be made? By what means of transportation? Who is to issue shipping instructions?

How are collections to be made? Is another batch of blankets to be made? When? And so on, in a never-ending cycle.

The foregoing summary does not by any means cover the list of decisions involved in the manufacture, sale, and distribution of 100,000 blankets, but they suffice to illustrate the network of questions which have to be decided, and it should be apparent that proper timing and harmony in these decisions is essential in order to have smoothly flowing, economical operations. The business can be a successful undertaking only when the blankets have been made and distributed and payment received sufficient to show a profit. A blanket on the bed of a consumer is the result not only of the physical processing of certain raw materials but of a vast network of administrative decisions.

It is the task of the chief executive to make the key decisions and to make sure that the supplementary decisions are made in due time, in proper sequence, and in harmony with the key decisions. His real authority is measured by the degree to which his key decisions are implemented by the supplementary decisions and actions of the rest of the organization.

An executive of a business corporation operates in an environment abounding in uncertainties. He seldom can know for sure in advance what will be the reactions of employees, customers, investors, creditors, and others to any course of action which it is decided to follow. In many industries, technological changes are continually taking place, and new economic, political, and social developments arise with perplexing frequency. Executive decisions often have to be reached before all the pertinent facts can be ascertained and before future trends can be fully evaluated. The wheels seldom can be stopped to await the gathering of more facts and the unfolding of new trends.

If the corporation has a well-chosen board of directors, the board determines policies and gives counsel and advice to the chief executive. Nevertheless, he must take the responsibility of putting the policies into effect. And on his shoulders rests a heavy responsibility for attaining successful results. Since he usually operates amidst so many uncertainties, mistakes in judgment inevitably occur. The executive has the authority to make mistakes. His success is measured, not by the infrequency with which he makes mistakes, but by the degree to which his sound decisions outweigh his faulty ones.

Finally, it should be pointed out that the task of making executive decisions in an environment so full of uncertainty and so fraught with actual or potential conflicts of interest places a burden on an executive which can be borne successfully only by a man of good physical stamina, intellectual honesty, and moral courage.

A college president once remarked to me that he did not rate highly the intellectual quality of many successful business executives. His remark was intended, in part, I judged, to needle me as a teacher in the field of business administration. He, like many another classicist, was disposed to look down his nose at the upstart business schools. But his remark also was at least partially serious. He meant, I took it, that he did not believe that numerous successful business executives had the capacity to write scholarly Ph.D. theses, for example. Had I chosen to enter into an argument, I would have pointed out that that particular capacity was not especially important in administrative work. I might also have pointed out that not all college presidents are eminent scholars, but that does not seriously lessen their competency for performing their administrative tasks. The competent administrator, furthermore, has qualities which are not possessed by many eminent scholars, and the qualities of the competent administrator are no less easy of attainment than the quality of scholarship. There are wide ranges of ability in both fields as well as in other types of human activity.

This chapter may well be concluded with the following quotation from M. Vachée in his study, *Napoleon at Work*. The analogy to industrial administration, it seems to me, is quite apparent.

> To keep incessantly in mind the material and moral situation of his army, to discover, from information which is often vague and contradictory the conditions and plans of the enemy, with these

uncertain data to arrive at a decision and carry it out without loss of time, to guard against the unexpected, to husband and accumulate his forces, so as to use them unsparingly at the decisive hour — such, in the main, is the role of a general-in-chief . . .

First of all, the work of a commander-in-chief calls for thought, preliminary to any decision. An idea is born, evolves, becomes well-defined, and by an act of will is transformed into a decision. But the role of a leader does not end here; he must also participate in the carrying of the decision into execution, by superintending, directing, and controlling his agents. This participation is indispensable to the union and consequence of their efforts, the rectification of errors, and the vigour of the action. Finally, the duty of a chief is also to distribute to the executants the rewards or penalties which correspond to their merit or their incapacity.

Every command, if exercised completely, is subject to these various obligations: intellectual work, the arrival at a decision, the superintendence of its execution, and the distribution of rewards and penalties.[4]

[4] J.B.M.E. Vachée, *Napoleon at Work,* translated from the French by G. Frederick Lees (London, 1914), pp. 1, 2.

II

The Executive's Lieutenants

The executive's lieutenants include department heads, staff officers, and other topside members of the administrative and supervisory organization. These lieutenants participate in the management of the enterprise and facilitate its operations. These lieutenants oftentimes also generate some of the executive's greatest perplexities. In this chapter some of the major problems pertaining to the executive's lieutenants are taken up, under the following headings: why have lieutenants?; executive job specifications; the man in the middle; relationships of lieutenants to each other; and, if competent lieutenants are employed, what is there left for the chief executive to do?

Why have lieutenants?

The employment of executive lieutenants represents a division of the labor of management. For successful management it is essential that the right decisions be made at the right time. Decisions, in other words, must be made competently and with proper timing. When a business grows beyond the stage where one man can effectively make all the administrative decisions, lieutenants normally are employed to aid the chief executive in the making and carrying out of competent and timely decisions.

The executive's lieutenants constitute the key men in the organization, and the question as to the why of having lieutenants therefore goes to the elements of organization. The following situations illustrate some of the reasons for the development of an organization in a business enterprise.

The simplest type of business is the small shop or store in which the proprietor himself makes all the decisions. If the enterprise expands beyond say a dozen employees, however, the proprietor usually finds it necessary to employ one or more department heads, foremen, or other assistants to whom the responsibility for making certain types of decisions is delegated. As further expansion takes place, more lieutenants are added. As Mr. Lawler has stated: "By the time a [manufacturing] company reaches the size of about 250 employees, it usually has an organization in which all the major functions are represented by specialists." [1]

When a business grows to a size where the proprietor does not have the time to make all the administrative decisions himself, he faces a crucial test. Does he have the ability to select and guide a group of department heads and other lieutenants? Can he delegate to a corps of lieutenants the responsibilities for managing specified activities, granting to each lieutenant decision-making responsibilities within a designated jurisdiction? Can he assign advisory functions to other members of a staff and then utilize the results of their work effectively in directing the activities of the operating departments?

The success of many a small business enterprise leads ultimately to its failure. Many a man, who can successfully direct operations when he is on the floor of the shop, does not have the managerial ability to enable him to pick and instruct

[1] Paul F. Lawler, *Records for the Control of Growing Manufacturing Enterprises* (Boston: Division of Research, Harvard Business School, 1947), p. 8.

lieutenants and thus lead an organization. The failure of many small business enterprises, which frequently show initial success, is attributable to a lack of elementary managerial abilities on the part of the founders.

Vigorous, growing enterprises, many of which must be started on a small scale, are essential to a healthy national economy. Thereby decadent enterprises are supplanted and therefrom come expanding opportunities for employment and widening facilities for the better satisfaction of consumers' wants. Opportunities for developing new enterprises, furthermore, provide an incentive to individual efforts which constitutes a powerful social leaven. An enterprise normally cannot continue to grow and prosper, however, unless it is well managed, an elementary fact which is often overlooked by political protagonists of "small business" who seek legislative panaceas for curing problems which can be solved only by improved managerial skill.

When an enterprise expands gradually, lieutenants can be added one by one by forming specialized departments and by splitting up operating departments as the scale of operations and other circumstances warrant it. If expansion takes place rapidly, however, the task of splitting up the administrative job and yet maintaining teamwork between the various operating and staff departments is a highly challenging one. Probably the most dramatic example of that type of experience occurred in the aircraft manufacturing industry during the Second World War. The five leading wartime airframe manufacturers, for example, averaged less than 1,400 employees each in 1935 and over 100,000 each in 1943. One of the near miracles of industrial production during that war

[2] Tom Lilley, Pearson Hunt, J. Keith Butters, Frank F. Gilmore, and Paul F. Lawler, *Problems of Accelerating Aircraft Production During World War II* (Boston: Division of Research, Harvard Business School, 1946), p. 58. The problems of providing management for the mushrooming industry are discussed at length in that report.

was the effective expansion of the administrative organizations of the aircraft manufacturing companies. This expansion was not accomplished without tribulation and grief, because executives who had been accustomed to working in small groups, intimately acquainted with each other, and able to exercise visual supervision over the progress of work on the floor of the shop, suddenly found the size of their groups multiplied manyfold, scattered in branch plants, with little chance for full personal acquaintance, and with formal procedures necessarily superseding informal practices. Seldom has executive ability in industry been put to such a grueling test.

One of the keys to effective organization is the avoidance or elimination of administrative bottlenecks, a fact well illustrated in this wartime expansion of the American aircraft industry. Any enterprise becomes paralyzed if there are persistently long or chronically occurring delays in the making of executive decisions. Such delays in executive decisions cause wasteful interruptions of operations and jeopardize the spirit of teamwork. Oftentimes, furthermore, it is less important that the decision made be the best possible decision than that *some* decision be made. Usually it is easier to correct a mistake than it is to regain lost momentum.

An administrative bottleneck may occur either because of the ineptitude of an executive himself or because of the incompetency of a lieutenant. For example, a heavy additional load was thrown upon the head of a department in a small organization. Whereas he previously had handled his duties competently, he seemed quite unable to cope with the task of making a much larger number of decisions. The work backed up, and he was becoming swamped, to the detriment of the whole enterprise. He was furnished an assistant, but that proved to be no solution; the department head did not have the knack of utilizing an assistant; decisions still were deferred; and complaints increased. Eventually the chief executive was reluctantly forced to the conclusion that the job was too big for that department head, and he was replaced. A bottleneck caused by incompetency can be relieved only by replacement.

Provided the executive and his lieutenants are competent, the occurrence of an administrative bottleneck or the threat of such a bottleneck points toward a further division of the labor of management. This is accomplished either by splitting off a part of the administrative job where the bottleneck impends and appointing a new lieutenant to handle that work, or by furnishing more administrative assistance at a lower level.

The avoidance of administrative bottlenecks is one purpose in having executive lieutenants. Another closely related purpose is to make it possible for the executive to concern himself with problems which do not have to be decided today. Not all executives, of course, take that view of their jobs. A high-pressure executive, for example, who sits at a desk with a battery of telephones and with several secretaries continually darting in and out of his office is busy, very busy. He is making decisions and keeping the wheels turning. But oftentimes that type of executive does not have time to think of problems which are not immediately urgent but which are more important than some of the current questions to which he is devoting attention.

The following statement by President Lowell was made with reference to university administration, but it is applicable also to business administration. He stated: "If the administrator feels tired or hurried it means that he is doing too much, that he has not learned that his business is thinking, not routine, and hence to put off until tomorrow the routine things that must be done today, and do today the things that can be done any day, for they are the important ones. If it does not mean this it means that the time has come to pass the work into younger hands."[3]

Thus executive achievement requires, among many other things, provision for promptness and competency in reaching decisions on questions which can be decided with short deliberation, and also promptness and competency in starting consideration of questions for which immediate answers cannot wisely be attempted. Except for occasional emergency situations, the questions which can be handled with short deliberation should as a general practice be ones for which policies have been set or precedents established and which therefore can be left for action by lieutenants with a minimum of risk. On the other hand, the questions to which immediate answers cannot wisely be attempted but to which answers will have to be found in the future belong primarily to the chief executive. Some of the executive's lieutenants, particularly those in staff departments, may be able to contribute to the consideration of such questions by assembling facts and furnishing suggestions. After such a question has been crystallized, furthermore, it may be one to be submitted to the board of directors. But it is the task of the executive to make the crystallization and, if possible, at least to suggest a proper course of action.

Every executive decision sets a policy or has policy-setting implications. The questions for which immediate answers cannot wisely be attempted typically involve long-range policy considerations; hence the importance attached to their being given deliberate attention by the executive. Leadership implies that the leader knows whither he is going.

For an executive to be in a position where he can give

[3] A. Lawrence Lowell, *What a University President Has Learned* (New York: Macmillan, 1938), p. 20.

thoughtful attention to long-range problems, he must have an organization of lieutenants who can take care of many of those questions which must be decided from hour to hour.

Executive job specifications

The appointment of a lieutenant to a position carrying a certain title does not automatically define his job. If that definition is not made by the chief executive, the job becomes defined in practice by the lieutenant himself, and his concept may not meet the needs of the company or be conducive to a high degree of teamwork. Several years ago when a new president was brought into a leather tanning company, he proceeded to revamp the sales organization by assigning a definite geographical territory to each salesman. Previously each salesman had had his own list of customers and prospective customers selected largely without reference to geographical location, with resultant crisscrossing of each other's routes by the salesmen. The new president, however, did not similarly define the administrative tasks of each department head. The result was that the chief chemist assumed some of the duties which properly belonged to the superintendent of production, the controller undertook to do some of the managing of sales, and other confused overlappings took place. The president was aiming at obtaining the best ideas from every source in his organization, a meritorious objective of course, but his failure to differentiate between means of getting ideas and of having them tried out only led to confusion. Furthermore, some highly important administrative areas were neglected because they were not specifically assigned to any one department head. Definition of administrative "territories" was even more necessary than delimitation of salesmen's geographical territories.

One of the main tasks of an executive is to obtain what I like to call teamwork among the members of his organization.

"Teamwork," in the sense in which I am using the term, includes the efficient working together of all the members of the administrative force, whether in span or in tandem, to attain the common goals of the undertaking for which they have been employed. And real teamwork can be attained only when each man on the team knows what his assignment is and undertakes to carry it out.

Trouble is in the making for such a situation as the following. A new president took over the management of a smallish company in which designing of the product was of especial importance. No special design department had been set up, and the responsibility for product designing had not been carefully placed. The production department and the sales department each was engaging in some product-designing activities, with a substantial amount of overlapping. The sales manager was ambitious and aggressive. The production manager was competent but reserved, and he strongly resented what he considered to be the administrative poachings of the sales manager. The new president chose not to make any immediate move, pending his attainment of greater familiarity with the affairs of the company. Meanwhile the sales manager was assuming more prerogatives, and the production manager was becoming more resentful. Teamwork between the two department heads on all matters was virtually at a standstill.

In another instance, a new president was brought in to be the head of a large company which had recently lost its chief executive through death. The new president, after he had been in office for a period of about six months, requested and obtained the approval of the board of directors for the employment of a firm of management consultants to examine the company's administrative organization with a view to revamping it. Eventually the consultants came up with a new set of executive job specifications which plugged one gaping hole in the organization and clarified the hitherto somewhat nebulous assignments of each department head. In putting the recommendation into effect the president found it necessary to make some modifications in the consultants' program, but he had a specific statement from which to work. The modifications did not lessen the clarity of the job specifications.

The foregoing examples have illustrated the need for defining each lieutenant's job. If used mechanically, however, such definitions can lead to rigidities and bureaucracies fully as destructive as the conditions which they seek to remedy. They can kill initiative, cause jurisdictional disputes, wreck teamwork, and leave administrative gaps uncovered. Executive job specifications, in fact, are a starting point rather than an end in administration. They have to be modified by year-to-year experience and by the exigencies of continually changing conditions.

The following experience, while it occurred twenty-odd years ago, illustrates the problem of adjustment to changing conditions. The company, with headquarters in upper New York State, manufactured a well-known grocery product. For marketing purposes the United States was divided into five sales divisions, each with a clearly specified territory. Each territorial sales manager was granted considerable leeway within his territory, with the result that some differences in terms of sale developed between the divisions. These differences averaged out, so that the net profit of each sales division was about the same as that of the other divisions. In the 1920's chain-store grocery companies and so-called voluntary chains expanded to a point where each of several chains was operating in three or more of this manufacturer's sales divisions. Then the chain-store buyers began to demand from the manufacturer for all their stores the best terms granted in any one district. This destroyed the old averaging-out process, to the disadvantage of the manufacturer. Consequently, the president of the company in 1929 called the division sales managers together and with the aid of a consultant undertook to standardize the sales terms for all divisions, so that one no longer could be played off against the others. Changes in retailing methods forced the president of the manufacturing company to redefine the decision-making jurisdiction of the divisional sales managers to accord with a standardized program. Incidentally, all the divisional sales managers readily agreed in principle to the adoption of standardized sales terms, but each was disappointed, some bitterly disappointed, when not all his pet terms were incorporated in the standard program. In fact, one of the divisional managers called the consultant immoral for not recommending that his pet policy be made standard.

Analogous examples which show the need for continual readjustment of executive jobs as conditions change are to be found in every thriving enterprise. These readjustments are essential functions for a chief executive who has the delicate task of maintaining an administrative equilibrium in a constantly changing environment.

The man in the middle

The department head is a lieutenant of the executive. A lieutenant receives instructions from above informing him as to his administrative jurisdiction and indicating the policies to be followed. Acting in accordance with those instructions, he is expected to secure effective results within his department. At the same time, the department head also is an emissary from the members of his department to the powers above him. He is a man in the middle, subject to pressures from both directions.

The man in the middle, therefore, has to be adaptable — adaptable to making decisions, to functioning as a subordinate, and to providing leadership for those under his command.

For many men the task of making decisions is not an easy one. They have an inherent aversion to taking such responsibilities. They have much in common with the Swede who was hired to sort apples in an apple-shipping station. The job was explained to him. He was to sort the apples into three lots: (1) perfect, (2) bruised, and (3) rotten. A couple of days after he started work, however, he went to the office and announced that he was quitting. He was asked why. "Isn't the pay all right?" "Yah, fine." "Aren't the hours satisfactory?" "Yah, o.k." "Isn't it a comfortable place to work?" "Yah, o.k." "Well, what's wrong? Why are you quitting?" "Ah have to make too gor damn many decisions."

The problems of adaptation to serving as a subordinate have been illustrated with especial force many times in the case of mergers. In 1899 and 1900, for example, many industrial combinations, as mergers were then called, were formed, and again in the 1920's another flock of mergers took place. Occasional mergers have been carried through in other periods. A high percentage of these mergers have not been successful, and one of the most common factors in nonsuccess has been the obstacles to securing teamwork from the former owners or chief executives of the various units when they were retained in the new organization and placed in subordinate positions.

Although not universally the practice in the formation of mergers, the former owners or chief executives of the merged companies often were taken on to manage the units which they formerly had headed or to assume some other executive positions. Indeed many of the mergers would not have gone through if the head men had not been assured that they would have jobs in the new organization. The previous owners and chief executives, however, seldom were effective as branch managers or as departmental officers. Having served as chief executives, they found it difficult to function again as subordinates. For them the acceptance of instructions from superior executives, particularly with reference to managing units which they felt themselves fully competent to manage without instructions from above, was damaging to their pride and their judgment. They had in effect been demoted in the administrative hierarchy and for them the stresses and strains of the readjustment militated strongly against their being able to function efficiently as members of the team.

Although a department head is a lieutenant of the executive for administration, he also is the channel through which the views of the departmental administrative staff and of the rank and file of employees are funneled upward to top management. When dissatisfaction with top management policies causes unrest among the rank and file, the department head really is a man in the middle. The dissatisfaction may stem from a lack of understanding of the policies, from delays in decision, or from questionable policies. Whatever the cause, in those circumstances the department head is under pressure from within the department to secure remedial action even though he may be powerless to influence his boss.

A department head, to be successful, must enjoy the confidence and support of his superior. Without that confidence and support, he cannot function as a real lieutenant. A department head also must earn the confidence and support of those who work under his supervision. As at all other stages in the administrative scale, a department head receives a grant of authority from his superior, but that grant is little more than an opportunity for him to achieve leadership within his sphere of command. An arrogant or inept lieutenant can be sabotaged or "broken" by those in his command. The sales girls in a department store, for example, can and sometimes do "break" an unpopular "buyer." Recently another example came to my attention. A young man of promise was made manager of one of the sales divisions of a large manufacturing company. Initially he had the confidence and support of his superior. Because of a certain lack of decisiveness in his work, however, he failed to gain the confidence of the salesmen of whom he was in charge. Morale slumped, and he had to be replaced. He could not be relied upon as a strong link in the administrative chain.

A department head who can successfully attain leadership of the personnel of his department while at the same time carrying out his instructions is a true teamworker. As a man in the middle of the organization, he holds a key position on the team.

Relationships of lieutenants to each other [4]

Many of the questions which come up for administrative decisions within a department have interdepartmental ramifications. The interdepartmental ramifications are adjusted principally in either of two ways. When a new problem arises involving major interdepartmental relationships, it properly goes to a higher executive for decision, his decision being binding on each of the departments involved. Numerous other interdepartmental problems are disposed of by mutual agreement between the department heads, either on the basis of the precedents established by earlier top management decisions, or in accordance with a preponderating weight of evidence after an interchange of information.

A generous interchange of information between department heads and the settlement of routine problems by mu-

[4] For a much more comprehensive explanation of the human relations in topside business administration, see Edmund P. Learned, David N. Ulrich, and Donald R. Booz, *Executive Action* (Boston: Division of Research, Harvard Business School, 1951).

tual agreement between them constitute a large fraction of the administrative teamwork in an organization. When one department head habitually "plays his cards close to his chest," however, refusing to divulge information to other department heads and acting independently in so far as his instructions permit him to do so, teamwork in the organization is at a minimum.

The interrelationships of lieutenants become complicated, moreover, as specialized staff departments are added to an organization and when multiple production or sales units are set up. Such complications are illustrated by the following examples.

A shoe manufacturing company, which had been making a poor financial showing, employed a cost analyst—he would have been called a cost accountant in many companies. It was the task of the cost analyst to estimate the cost of production for each lot of shoes as the orders came in and later to compare the actual costs with the estimated costs. When the actual costs were in excess of the estimated costs, as they only too frequently were, the cost analyst went to the foremen who were responsible for the costs that were out of line and sought to obtain corrective action. The cost analyst accomplished little, for he had no disciplinary power over the foremen. That is a very common type of administrative experience. Instead of being permitted to attempt to secure corrective action by short circuit, the cost analyst should have been instructed to furnish the information to the superintendent of production, who in turn would have been expected to induce the foremen to mend their ways or to find other means of bringing production costs into line. This experience illustrates one of the most elementary principles of organization, namely that a member of one department cannot exercise disciplinary control over the members of another department.

In the instance just cited, the superintendent of production might have objected to the estimates of the cost analyst, on the grounds that they were inaccurate. If the superintendent of production and the cost analyst could not have agreed as to the facts, the case would have been one for arbitration by the chief executive.

In the foregoing instance, the chief executive had failed to define fully the job of the cost analyst and to acquaint the other department heads with the working arrangements. The chief executive presumably had made the oft-repeated mistake of assuming that if he provided a "system," the desired improvement would take place. A similarly erroneous assumption often has been made when budgets or other "systems" were introduced.

The foregoing example involved line and staff relationships. In general it may be stated that a staff department is set up for the purpose of providing the chief executive and the heads of the operating departments with specialized assistance, as in the case of the legal, engineering, and research departments; of relieving the chief executive of part of his burden, by analyzing and studying operations and problems, in order to provide him with information which will enable him to reach sound conclusions more expeditiously; and of relieving the heads of operating departments or branches of tasks which can be performed more economically or more effectively, or both, by one central department serving several operating departments. This splitting off of specialized staff functions, however, gives rise to some of the most perplexing problems of executive leadership, because of the manner in which it complicates the relationships of the executive's lieutenants to each other.

While discussing this subject of staff departments with me a few years ago, a business executive of wide experience remarked that when a staff officer finds a situation which needs to be corrected in a line department, the temptation for him to attempt to do something about it directly himself is often almost overwhelming, even though he knows that such action on his part is likely to make matters worse. The president of another company who was present stated that in his company's written regulations of standard practice he had incorporated a rule that a staff man may confer with a subordinate in a line department only in the presence of the subordinate's line officer. The purpose of that rule was to avoid confusion of instructions to subordinates and to minimize the loopholes for alibis.

The relationships between line officers and staff officers also are complicated in some instances by the circumstances that many staff officers are specialists. Indeed, one of the chief reasons for setting up certain staff departments, such as the legal department, the accounting department, the engineering department, and the medical department, is to facilitate the employment of functional specialists. The specialist usually has been trained in the techniques of his specialty, and his concentrated technical training has not included indoctrination in administrative methods or in the administrative point of view. On technical questions, the specalized staff officer obviously has an advantage over his fellow line officers who are laymen. On administrative matters, the specialized staff officer frequently is at a disadvantage.

The problem of finding technical specialists sufficiently competent in administration to function effectively as executive lieutenants is a very real one.[5] Among technical specialists administrative ability is rare, and certain types of technical specialists have little regard for such mundane

[5] For further discussion of this subject, see T. F. Bradshaw, *Developing Men for Controllership* (Boston: Division of Research, Harvard Business School, 1950).

nuisances as budgets and time schedules. Sometimes, in selecting a department head, a choice has to be made between a scientist who is not an administrator and an administrator who is not a scientist. In such a situation my experience indicates that the administrator is likely to be the better bet. He can be supported by technically trained assistants. Many decisions which must be made by the head of a technical staff department involve not only technical questions but also major problems of interdepartmental relationships, and there administrative ability is essential. It is a heterogeneous team, to put it mildly, which typically a chief executive must lead.

The interrelationships between executive lieutenants are further complicated by the distance factor when branch operations are undertaken. As an example the experience can be cited of a baking company operating seventeen plants located in cities up to seven hundred miles distant from the city where the main office was situated. These decentralized production operations facilitated prompt delivery of fresh bakery products to retailers in the localities where the company operated. Each plant was large enough to operate economically, and from a production cost and sales standpoint decentralization was advantageous. From an administrative standpoint, however, decentralization of operations gave rise to troublesome problems.

The president of that baking company had the administrative assistance of eight staff officers and seventeen branch managers. The staff officers included the treasurer, controller, purchasing agent, bread production manager, cake production manager, advertising manager, sales manager, and equipment manager. In each branch, under the branch manager, were superintendents of bread production, cake production, equipment, sales, accounting, and local purchasing.

The branch manager was the focus of the administrative

problem in that case. In order to realize the advantages of decentralized production and delivery and to maintain orderliness in operations, it was necessary to have a manager of each branch plant. It was not easy, however, to define workable relationships between the branch manager and the staff at headquarters and to determine what decisions were within the jurisdiction of the branch manager and what decisions were to be made by the headquarters staff. If each branch manager was to be entirely free, there was no need for any headquarters staff; if the branch manager had no freedom of choice, he could make no decisions in accordance with the needs of the local situation. If the branch manager could overrule instructions to his superintendents from the headquarters staff, the influence of that staff officer would be impaired. If he could not control his superintendents, he could not be held responsible for successful operation of the branch.

It was essentially the same problem which caused some of the worst administrative headaches, or should one say administrative ulcers, in the American aircraft manufacturing industry when it expanded its operations so rapidly in the Second World War. At the war's end some of the large aircraft manufacturing companies had not attained fully satisfactory working arrangements between the headquarters staffs and the manager of branch plants located in various parts of the United States. In at least one of the largest companies, the turnover of branch managers during the war was very high. In the hurly-burly of demands for ever-increasing production schedules, technological developments, labor and material shortages, and other complications, time was not taken to face some of the elementary administrative problems, particularly those of establishing fully workable administrative arrangements between the staffs at headquarters and the managers of branch plants and their staffs.

In still other fields the same basic problem appears. Some of the grocery chain-store companies which have replaced the smaller stores with much larger units known as supermarkets are finding that profits are shrinking, at least temporarily. Apparently one of the causes for the less satisfactory earnings is the difficulty of fitting the managers of the supermarkets effectively and economically into the administrative hierarchy of the chain.

In the small store operated by a chain, the store manager was little more than a head salesman. He had been relieved largely of such tasks as buying, pricing, accounting, finance, and advertising. Those matters were taken care of for him at headquarters. He was responsible to a district manager who in turn reported to a division manager. That was a simple administrative setup. When a chain-store company shifted to the operation of supermarkets, however, with large departments in each store, as for example one for dry groceries, one for meats, and one for fruits and vegetables, a new administrative setup was needed. Then the chain-store company found itself in a situation quite analogous to that in the bakery and aircraft industries just cited. The chain operating supermarkets likewise had to harmonize a three-dimensional organization, consisting of functional and line department heads at central headquarters, line supervisors, store managers, and department heads in the stores. In such a situation it is by no means easy to avoid confusion as to lines of authority and responsibility.

In the department store field, some of the large firms which have opened branches likewise are finding it difficult to define in workable terms the job of a branch manager in his relations to his staff and in relation to the staff and line department heads at the main store.

Presumably something of the same sort has arisen in the

coal-mining industry in England since it was nationalized, as indicated in the following quotation:

> For example, the virtues of nationalization, long one of Labor's major goals, have been called into question by the experiences of the coal-mining industry since the National Coal Board took over on "vesting day," January 1, 1947. One unexpected result has been the lack of any real improvement in the morale of the miner. Nationalization has not brought workers' control; the national and divisional boards, the area and colliery officials, are the old directors and officers writ large — and in the higher levels made more remote and impersonal. Shorter hours, higher wages, more mechanization have increased costs without greatly increasing output, even though everything is done to bring home to the miner the fact that greater production is vital to the survival of the nation; he works no harder for the public good than he did for private profit. At the same time, nationalization has brought to the fore the problem of administration: can an industry so large and varied be managed from London, and if so, what pattern of organization will permit authority to be delegated, lines of communication kept clear, and decisions given rapidly, without leading to such a confusion of policies and competition between areas or departments as would defeat the objects of centralization and over-all planning. At present the system has among its principal products an increase in the number of nonproducers in the industry, an unexpectedly high range of salaries for executives at headquarters, and a feeling of frustration on the part of many colliery managers and production officials who must serve many masters and endure long delays while waiting for rulings on points large and small.[6]

Given time and a continuity of leadership under an executive with a steady hand, an intelligent mind, and a knack of sympathetic administration, effective working relationships between line and staff officers can be worked out, even when the distance factor enters into the complications. Such a

[6] C. L. Mowat, "British Socialism: Pitfalls and Prospects," *American Scholar* (Autumn 1949), p. 398.

development, however, does not come about easily and automatically.

The foregoing statements by no means fully cover the problems of interrelationships between the executive's lieutenants, but they do present some of the considerations. Further examples will be cited in subsequent chapters.

At this point a somewhat parenthetical observation also may be in order. In my experience, one of the most widespread fallacies encountered in economics and business pertains to the assumed economies of large-scale operations. For more than fifty years, at least, there has been an almost blind acceptance in many quarters of inadequately supported theories regarding economies of large size. Some large enterprises obviously are highly successful; others are not successful. In the economic and financial discussions of the economies of large-scale operations, inadequate attention almost invariably is given to key administrative questions, examples of some of which have just been cited.

If competent lieutenants are employed, what is there left for the chief executive to do?

It would not have occurred to me to ask this question, were it not for an experience with a student which led to some experiments which, for me at least, were enlightening. As has often happened in the use of the case method of instruction over a period of years, I uncovered in this instance something which eventually appeared to be a fairly common blind spot among the students.

In the winter of 1940 a student came to my office to clear up certain points in a case which we had had up for discussion in the Administrative Policy class that day. After reviewing the diagnosis, and finally concluding that there was need for a defining of the jobs of all the department heads and for plugging several holes in the organization, the student unexpectedly asked: "If Mr. Edgerton [the president] adds those men to the staff, and has a properly qualified man at the head of each department, what is there left for him to do?"

After parrying the question a bit, I asked the student whether he were interested in baseball. He replied that he was. I then asked him whether there was anything left for Joe McCarthy to do, if he had a competent player in each position on the New York Yankee team which Mr. McCarthy was then managing. The analogy could not be pressed too far, of course, but it did serve to suggest an effective answer to that student's question.

As other students came in to talk over their problems, I took occasion to test out a number of them on the question as to whether there was anything left for the chief executive of a company to do once he had obtained a competent corps of lieutenants. I soon found that there was a rather common inability to answer that question.

In discussing the subject with the students, I sometimes repeated the query as to the management of a professional baseball team or a professional hockey team. In other instances I used various nonbusiness institutions as analogies. Then one day I encountered a Yale graduate who scorned professional athletics and had not been a member of a fraternity or any other organization except the Yale glee club. I might have taken the glee club for illustration, but my competency in music is so limited and my deficiencies in that subject had been commented on so frequently by members of my family, that I shifted to another analogy. I asked that student whether there was anything left for President Seymour of Yale to do, provided he had a competent dean at the head of each department and competent officers on the business staff. Of course, the question might have been phrased: "If President Seymour is a busy man, does that indicate that he has an incompetent administrative staff under him?"

A couple of days after my conversation with the Yale graduate, a student who had graduated from Harvard College was in my office and I decided to try him out. I asked him what there was left for President Conant to do if he had a competent man at the head of each administrative department of the university. To which the student immediately replied: "I have often wondered that myself."

The question as to what constitutes the executive's job has been answered in part, I trust, in these first two chapters. In the chapters which follow an attempt is made to provide a more comprehensive answer to that question.

III

Coaching the Lieutenants

In order to have a competent lieutenant in each key position in the organization, vacancies must be filled as they occur. Some turnover in an executive staff is inevitable. Vacancies arise out of natural causes, such as illness and death. They also arise out of dismissals resulting from earlier mistakes in selection and the failure of some men to live up to the promise which they showed at the time of appointment. As an enterprise enlarges the scope of its activities, furthermore, new executive lieutenants have to be provided. The selection of new lieutenants is one of the major tasks of a chief executive. Even though vacancies occur only at irregular intervals of some length, they do come frequently enough in most organizations to constitute ever-present contingencies.

Counsel and advice

When an executive has selected competent lieutenants, however, his task is not finished. In fact, it has only started. The lieutenants have to be welded into an "organization," a group working together as a team. They have to be furnished with directions and instructions. A new lieutenant, moreover, usually needs individual coaching[1] in order to enable him to

[1] See also Myles L. Mace, *The Growth and Development of Executives* (Boston: Division of Research, Harvard Business School, 1950), chap. vi.

realize his full potentialities. While he may have a natural aptitude for the position and a fertile background of experience, the position is new to him and any promotion almost inevitably involves personal readjustments. He cannot fairly be expected to understand intuitively what the job comprises and how it can best be handled. The better he has been trained in previous assignments, to be sure, the more readily may he be able to grasp his new tasks. Nevertheless, he does have to learn what the new job involves and how best to deal with the problems which it presents. The learning process can be speeded up by proper instruction and skillful coaching.

When a man brought in from outside to head a department has not held a similar position with a previous employer, he needs a training similar to that of a man promoted from within the company plus orientation on the company's organization and affairs. If a man brought in from outside has held a similar position elsewhere and is already trained, the education job has been done by someone else, perhaps a competitor. In such a situation as the latter one, reëducation sometimes is necessary. Ready-made lieutenants, well fitted to their jobs, are not easy to come by.

After the lieutenants have become firmly established in their positions, furthermore, individual situations are continually arising in which they need or desire counsel and advice from their superior officer. The providing of such counsel and advice is a significant part of the job of the executive who is responsible for getting things done.

Thus a major qualification for an executive position is an ability to teach — to coach an administrative team. In this respect the qualifications for serving as the chief executive of a business enterprise are analogous to the qualifications of a good football coach or those of a manager of a professional baseball team. Proficiency in executive leadership includes an ability to develop administrative proficiency in others.

For many positions, in business as well as in other activities, ability to teach as well as technical proficiency is a prerequisite to genuine achievement. Nevertheless, that elementary fact is overlooked, I am convinced from my own experience and observations, in an amazingly large number of cases. To emphasize this point I will cite several more examples from a variety of callings.

In 1948 a new coach was appointed for a certain college football team. As an undergraduate he had been an All-American halfback. After graduation he was a star player on one of the leading professional football teams for several years. He had demonstrated unusual technical competency as a player. Nevertheless he failed as a coach; he did not have the knack of imparting his own competency to others. That experience has been repeated time and time again in the coaching history of numerous colleges.

While referring to college experiences, furthermore, it may not be amiss to point out that many an eminent scholar has failed to achieve success as a college president. Likewise, a great scholar does not necessarily make a great dean. The academic world furnishes abundant and frequently unhappy evidence of the truth of these statements. Scholarly ability does not necessarily imply administrative ability or proficiency in developing administrative ability in others.

In the business field, during the Second World War, the executive of a large company in a long-established industry was elected president of a company in another industry which was expanding rapidly for the manufacture of military equipment on a very large scale. He had been highly successful in the enterprise where he grew up. In some respects he was successful in his wartime job. Nevertheless the stenographic records which were kept of staff meetings show that such success as he attained in the wartime job occurred in spite of a lack of ability on his part to train his lieutenants in handling some of their most basic relationships. In that instance the wartime pressures and the absence of competitive rivalry on a cost basis facilitated success despite a creaky organization. Under normal competitive conditions, the results probably would have been disastrous.

In another instance, at a meeting of business executives held during the war for a discussion of production problems, the question was asked: "What are you doing to educate foremen and shop stewards?" To that question the president of one company, employing several thousand workers, revealingly replied: "We are not running an educational institution. Our job is to turn out goods at as low a cost as possible."

That answer, in substance, was a glib alibi, but it also had far-reaching implications. While the question asked pertained to the training of foremen and shop stewards, the president's answer reflected his attitude toward his whole job of administration. From personal acquaintance with the affairs of the company, I know that there was a lack of teamwork in the organization, that some lieutenants were weak, that unit production costs were high rather than low, and that the company's earnings were poor except in boom years. While other factors, of course, affected the over-all results, one of the chief causes for the chronically poor earnings of the company was administrative ineptness. That ineptness did not arise from a lack of technical knowledge of production, finance, and sales, but rather from a lack of administrative "know-how" and from a dearth of ability to teach others the art of administration. Had that executive been a competent coach, the company itself might again have become a prosperous enterprise; instead it became a derelict.

Another very common situation in business is that of the

executive who is overloaded with detail work. Such an executive usually is one who does not know how or who is unwilling to take the time to teach subordinates to act effectively as his lieutenants.

The amazing thing about all these experiences is not that the able technical operator often lacks competency in training others; it is rather that so little about the importance of coaching ability has been learned from all these common experiences in the selection of executives and lieutenants, not only in business but in many other activities as well.

An effective executive need not be a schoolmaster, but he must be a teacher. If it is to progress and prosper in an ever changing world, a business enterprise must be an educational institution, and its leader an educator. The prosperity of a business concern is dependent far more on the abilities and aptitudes of the human beings who operate it than on the bricks and mortar in which it is housed or the machines which grind out the product. And the effective development of constructive abilities and aptitudes, which is an educational task, stems from leadership at the top.

Educability as a factor in the selection of a lieutenant

A candidate for selection as an executive lieutenant in a well-managed enterprise must possess certain qualities. His integrity, honesty, and sincerity must be beyond question. A lieutenant who does not have real integrity and who is not wholly honest and sincere cannot be expected to retain the loyalty and support of his subordinates. Moreover, a lieutenant who has a yellow streak cannot be fully relied upon in periods of stress and strain when the greatest organizational strength is needed. Integrity, honesty, and sincerity are qualities in which a man must rate 100% or zero. Unless a candidate can be rated 100%, it is futile to dream of educating him to raise his standards after appointment. Those are qualities with which he must have been endowed before appointment, not through education on the job.

Another essential quality for a lieutenant is "guts." There is no effective synonym for that inelegant word, and there is no substitute for that quality in administration. Unless a man has the courage and stamina to take responsibility, to make decisions, to face unpleasant situations when they arise, and to stand the consequences without flinching when he makes mistakes and errors of judgment, he cannot become an effective lieutenant. I have no scientific proof of this statement, but it is my conviction, for whatever it may be worth, that unless a man is born with "guts," he never has them. At all events I have found no means of developing them in a man who lacks them, and I doubt whether any amount of coaching will correct such a deficiency in a candidate for an executive lieutenancy.

Imagination and resourcefulness also are qualities possessed by a competent lieutenant. They, too, seem to me to be inherently native abilities, but they are not absolute values. Different men possess these qualities to varying degrees, and in some instances the native ability has not been developed. It may be latent. In such instances it may be nourished by wise guidance.

Inasmuch as an executive lieutenant is to be a member of an administrative team, his capacity for teamwork is another important consideration in making the selection. Some prospective candidates have a well-developed facility for working in a team. Others tend to "play their cards close to their chests" and to be noncoöperative. In some instances such a noncoöperative attitude is a manifestation of innate characteristics, and a candidate of that type is not likely to respond favorably to counsel and advice. In other instances such an attitude reflects earlier environmental influences and experiences rather than innate limitations, and in such a case the candidate may well be educable. In the last sort of case much depends on how long the souring process has been going on.

Technical qualifications commonly play an important part in the selection of department heads, as for example in the choice of an engineer to head an engineering department, an accountant to serve as controller, a man with a sales background for a sales managership, and a man with a factory experience to serve as production manager. Such technical qualifications must have been attained before, not after, appointment to an administrative post; in the bustle of administration there will be little opportunity for a new department head to undergo technical training. Nevertheless the technical proficiency, which may satisfy one requirement toward qualifying for a key administrative post, may constitute a handicap from another standpoint. A highly trained specialist, such as an engineer or an accountant, oftentimes lacks an aptitude for administration.[2] Indeed, his concentration on attaining technical proficiency may have had a narrowing effect, thereby lessening his ability to comprehend the problems of other departments and their interrelationship to his own special field. His concentration on attaining technical proficiency, furthermore, may have rendered him impatient with human problems of the type which bulk so large in administration.

Since it is rather rare to find a well-rounded candidate for an executive lieutenancy who is qualified on all counts, the choice often comes down to a selection of the man who seems most likely to be able to make up his deficiencies by learning on the job, with the aid of such coaching as may be available.

The philosophy of management exemplified in the foregoing statement, with all its implications, is by no means uni-

[2] On this subject, see T. F. Bradshaw, *Developing Men for Controllership* (Boston: Division of Research, Harvard Business School, 1950).

versally accepted. The following example illustrates another point of view. I have encountered other executives who professed an interest in this other point of view, but so far as I am aware none of them have put it into effect as thoroughly as was done in the following case.

Several years ago the president of a large textile manufacturing company announced that his purpose was to organize the departments in that company so that each department head would run his department as though he were in business for himself, standing on the record of the profit earned or falling on the loss incurred. That policy did not work out successfully, for it was basically unsound. For one thing, it militated against instead of encouraging teamwork between departments. It generated interdepartmental friction. It encouraged the taking of unwise chances because a department head actually was venturing the corporation's capital, not his own, and he was more ready to take long risks than he would have taken in a business of his own. Particularly significant was the fact that under that administrative policy the chief executive abjured effective control over the department heads and forewent any substantial opportunity for counseling and guiding them. Under that policy the department heads were not executive lieutenants, and the chief executive, in effect, was confessing to his inability to serve as a leader.

The supply of competent administrators available from which a choice can be made to fill vacancies in departmental managerial positions is influenced substantially by the policy which a company follows in selecting and training men in the lower administrative ranks. A good foreman, for example, is more than a highly skilled workman plus a title. A foreman has managerial duties to perform, and if foremen are chosen for their managerial aptitudes as well as for their technical ability, a beginning is made toward building a reserve of managerial manpower for higher positions. Foremen, moreover, need training, particularly for the development of managerial skills. Some of that training can be provided in formal classes, but all too frequently the most important type of effective foreman training is neglected, namely individual counsel and advice on managerial problems. Hence the division manager or superintendent has a responsibility for coaching foremen, and the division managers and superintendents in turn can benefit from counsel and advice from their superiors. Similar opportunities exist for training managerial manpower in other departments. Thus in a well-managed enterprise the whole administrative hierarchy is engaged in education, and the better the educational task is performed at all stages in that hierarchy, the greater will be the supply of competent administrative talent from which to choose men to fill the key positions as department heads when vacancies occur.

What is involved in coaching?

The first step in aiding an executive lieutenant to acquire mastery of his position is to define his job — to specify the managerial area within which he is to exercise his discretion in making decisions. If a new man is appointed sales manager, for example, is he to have responsibility for hiring and firing salesmen, or can he only make recommendations to his boss on such matters? Is he to fix rates and methods of compensation of salesmen? What jurisdiction is he to have over prices? Does he have the final decision on new items to be added to the line? These are a few of the questions involved in defining the managerial jurisdiction of a sales manager.

In the case of a personnel manager, to cite another example, some of the questions to which he needs the answers are the following. Do his activities embrace all the departments of the company, or only one department, such as the factory?

What is the jurisdiction of the personnel officer and that of the line officers in the hiring and firing of employees? Is the personnel manager to take part in negotiations with a labor union? If so, with what authority?

A proper definition of a lieutenant's job thus carries with it a substantial amount of instruction. Supplementary instruction of the same type is provided as new situations arise and as conditions change.

Another step, and one of the most important ones, in the education of department heads is the process of enlightening them on administrative policies. An administrative policy is a general rule of action which is developed, either formally or informally, for guiding the members of an administrative organization in deciding specific questions within their respective jurisdictions. In other words, an administrative policy is an instruction in principle as to how specific situations are to be dealt with. Where consistent policies have been developed which are really understood by the lieutenants, they can make decisions on specific questions substantially as those questions would be decided by the chief executive himself without having to place them before him. Thus the formulation of administrative policies and the instruction of the lieutenants so that they have a real understanding of those policies constitute a major function of executive leadership.

When a company is operated without clear-cut, well-understood policies, the result is confusion and frustration in the organization. For example, in the late 1930's, the executives of a certain company began to discuss possible changes in price policy. The company, although not large in comparison with some of the big American corporations, was by far the largest in its industry. It had had a long life and a good reputation. Nevertheless, for some years before the current question arose, the company had been experiencing difficulty in maintaining the volume of its sales. New schemes of warehousing, customer rebates, and so on had been tried, without effecting any marked improvement.

When the discussions of a possible new price policy were opened, a consultant was invited to sit in with the top executive group. At an early stage in the discussion, the consultant asked for the terms on which sales were made to certain large customers. It immediately appeared that there was complete disagreement among the executives present as to the answer to be made to that simple question. The lack of a clear-cut, well-understood policy on terms of sales unfortunately was symptomatic of the manner in which the company was being managed. It was small wonder that it was not flourishing.

To digress briefly, I might add that policies sometimes lack clarification even in educational institutions. Early in my academic career I served a brief term as instructor at another institution. In mid-fall a meeting of one of the faculties was held at which the new president of the institution was present. When the secretary of the faculty reported on student enrollment, which included a considerable number of "special" students, the president asked for an explanation of what constituted a "special" student and of the conditions on which "specials" were admitted. The secretary replied with a long, rather involved explanation, upon completion of which the president nodded and said that he understood. The dean, however, quickly remarked: "I don't. That is almost wholly contrary to what I understood our policy to be." Thereupon, the secretary gave a further, more involved explanation, which left everybody, including the president, thoroughly confused.

In business administration some policies are formulated by the board of directors and announced to the operating officials for their guidance. Many policies, or working rules, however, are evolved by the operating organization from the discussion of specific cases as they come up for decision. In the process of discussing concrete cases with his lieutenants, some of the most important coaching is done by an executive. In fact, his ability to utilize such opportunities effectively is one of the major tests of an executive as a coach.

This point was well illustrated by an experience which I had some twenty years ago. This experience occurred at a lower level in the organization but it involves the same principle and also shows how the opportunities for coaching arise everywhere within an administrative organization. I was questioning a sales manager of a certain company regarding the records and capabilities of the salesmen under his jurisdiction. When we came to one of the men, Bevis by name, the sales manager remarked that Bevis was not very competent, and pulled out of his desk some recent correspondence. Bevis had asked the sales manager for advice as to how to handle a situation such as he had just encountered with a department store buyer in St. Louis. The sales manager's reply was: "Tell that buyer that the next time I am in St. Louis I will come in to see him and straighten this out." By that statement the sales manager unwittingly revealed one of his own major weaknesses, an inability to grasp an opportunity to coach one of his men. Instead of taking the time to discuss the problem fully with the salesman in order to provide him with an understanding of how to handle such situations in the future, the sales manager through his brusqueness must have left the salesman with quite a chilly feeling.

The case method of instruction is widely and continuously in use in all well-managed organizations as a means of coaching lieutenants. By discussing with the lieutenants new problems as they arise, an executive helps them to gain a better understanding of the situations to be dealt with and precedents are established for the lieutenants to serve as future guides on policy questions.

The asking of searching questions is one of the devices successfully used by some executives in coaching their lieutenants. I am informed that one of the high executives in the United States government during the Second World War seldom issued an order or directive to his assistants. Instead he asked questions. As the answers came back, he confirmed them or asked more questions until he received an answer which he could confirm. Thus he educated his assistants to find solutions to their problems and enhanced the likelihood of their understanding the policies which they were expected to carry out.

Under some conditions committees also serve as a useful educational device to supplement individual coaching. In some instances they are particularly helpful as a means of interdepartmental education, to enable the several department heads to become better acquainted with each other's problems and to foster teamwork.

A whole volume, or perhaps several volumes, undoubtedly could be written on committees in administration, their advantages and their dangers, but I shall refer to them only briefly here, from an educational standpoint. It is to be recognized, of course, that standing committees and special committees in many organizations serve as means of gathering facts, crystallizing problems, and proposing courses of action for consideration by larger management groups. Such committees have considerable educational value to their members although their primary purpose is to facilitate administration. In some enterprises committees occasionally are appointed as a means of dodging or deferring decisions on annoying administrative problems. Committees also are appointed in some organizations chiefly to satisfy certain executives who just dote on attending committee meetings. But there are also numerous circumstances in which committees are utilized primarily for educational purposes.

Some of the situations in which committees have been

found useful as a means of education are the following. First, when there is an extensive change in executive personnel. Then a committee or series of committees can serve to acquaint the members with each other's problems and with their various approaches to their problems.

Second, when major changes in operations are contemplated, such as a large expansion of plant or a radical departure in the production and sale of new products. In such a situation a committee of key executives can enlighten themselves on the problems to be faced while planning the new operations. New points of view can thereby be developed, one of the most difficult tasks in education.

Third, when radically new conditions have to be faced. In 1944–45, for example, numerous companies had committees at work on postwar plans. In many a case the executives who served on such a committee not only contributed to the formulation of sound programs which stood their companies in good stead when the need arose, but they also gained a valuable perspective on the impending problems.

The foregoing situations by no means exhaust the list of opportunities for the educational use of committees, but they suffice to suggest the scope of opportunities for utilizing that device. A competent executive contributes to the work of such committees by posing at least some of the problems to be considered and by discussing with a committee the results of their deliberations.

Some general observations on coaching

Coaching is not hand-holding, or the providing of a crutch for lame ducks. It is a means of developing and strengthening potentially strong lieutenants. A good coach is continually observing his lieutenants to ascertain their weak points and seeking to ascertain how those weak points can be strengthened. He permits them to take responsibility and to make mistakes, with an expectation that by making mistakes they will become receptive to counsel and advice.

Several years ago I was chatting with the coach of a college football team which had just lost a game by a close score, even though on several occasions it had been close to the opponent's goal line. The coach remarked that he had not sent in instructions to the quarterback because, he said, "we might have won the game but ruined a potentially first class quarterback." The good coach knows when to put his pupil "on his own."

Patience and forbearance are essential qualities for an executive and a coach. He must be prepared to let his lieutenants make mistakes when he is confident that they can learn from such errors. After a mistake has been made, furthermore, a good coach patiently tries to help the man to attain an understanding of where he erred and how such mistakes can be avoided in the future. Much the same point was stated by William Knudsen, former president of General Motors Corporation, in an interview in 1941. He stated: "I found out a long time ago that if I yelled at a fellow, I'd scare him, and when he was scared he'd lie to me. If you're going to be a boss, it's your business to help out the fellows who are actually doing the work, and if they're scared, they just won't tell you their troubles." [3] That last sentence contains much of the gist of coaching.

Patience also is necessary because real education is a slow process. Books can be read and words memorized by youthful prodigies without their attaining any real understanding of the content and meaning of what they have studied. Lieutenants also can read directives and listen to instructions without really understanding them. It is the task of the boss to make sure that the policies to be followed are understood by his lieutenants. I suppose that one reason why the mak-

[3] *Life* (March 31, 1941), p. 114.

ing of mistakes so often is helpful to the educational process is that thereby the receptivity to instruction is substantially increased.

In administration, a good coach is a good listener. Hence one of the first requirements is for an executive to organize his work so that ordinarily he is available on short notice for consultation and advice. I have observed that when a lieutenant can readily obtain access to the boss and can have an opportunity to state any problems that are troubling him and to explain any suggestions which he has to offer, morale is substantially better than in those situations where it usually is difficult to see the boss or to have enough time to talk things over with him in an atmosphere of relaxation.

When a chief executive either is temperamentally too impatient to listen to his lieutenants or cannot organize his affairs so as to have time to listen to them, a substitute procedure is sometimes workable. The president of one large institution, for example, has so many demands on his time for other purposes and temperamentally is such an impatient listener that he has turned over to a right-hand man much of the conferring with other lieutenants. The right-hand man is a good listener, and at least some of the lieutenants find this arrangement quite a satisfactory one. Many a person is much more concerned with having an opportunity to talk about his problems than he is with what action finally is taken on them. Listening is an essential counterpart of coaching.

The executive who is a coach receives as well as gives education. Any good teacher must constantly be learning. The educational process for a real teacher is never complete and each experience enriches his background or improves his techniques. A capable lieutenant, furthermore, assumes a certain responsibility for educating his boss, unobtrusively of course. By the reports which he submits and by the questions which he raises, a lieutenant can direct somewhat the thinking of his boss. Administration in all its aspects is a two-way road, and this applies to the educational process as well as to other aspects of administration.

In conclusion, it may not be wholly amiss for me to refer to a couple of personal experiences in being coached. When I entered Harvard as a graduate student in economics I elected to take Professor Taussig's seminar course and began a study of the cotton manufacturing industry. Early in my second year I made an oral report to the seminar on some of my findings. As I walked homeward with Professor Taussig after the meeting, he suggested that I write up my material with a view to possible publication. I replied that I already had it in written form, and he indicated that he would like to look it over. Several weeks later the manuscript was returned to me with editorial comments in red ink which took up almost more space than the original text. I knew beforehand that I was not a skilled writer, but until I received Professor Taussig's unsparing but constructive criticism I was not aware how much I still had to learn about the use of the English language. Professor Taussig was a very busy man, but he was also a very kindhearted man and an excellent teacher. He taught me then an invaluable lesson.

The other experience to which I will refer was with Professor Gay, the first dean of the Harvard Business School. I had been invited to return to the school in the fall of 1912 as an instructor to start a course in Business Statistics and also to participate in the instruction in a course then known as "Commercial Organization," a course which two years later we decided to call Marketing. On Monday evening, the day of registration, Dean Gay informed me that because of an increase in enrollment "Commercial Organization" was to be divided into two sections. Professor Paul T. Cherington was to handle one section; I was to teach the other, starting on Wednesday at 9 A.M. — thirty-six hours' advance notice for teaching a course with which I had only a vague acquaintance and little background. Ten days later I encountered Dean Gay on the steps in front of his study as I was returning from my class. He asked how it was going, to which I replied: "I have found enough to talk about so far." "Hmph!" was the Dean's rejoinder, "that is not the question. Have you found enough to keep the students talking?"

That question was a jolter. As I soon discovered, there is a vast difference between lecturing and attempting to lead an effective discussion. A lecturer can pass over, with little or no reference, points on which he is not well informed. When a problem is opened up for discussion by the students, however, the teacher must expect that points will be brought up and questions raised to which he will have to admit that he does not know the answer. The discussion method, I have long been convinced, is the better educational procedure but it is substantially harder on the teacher.

Dean Gay was striving to have the instruction in the new school developed, so far as possible and as rapidly as possible, on the basis of discussion, a basis which subsequently became known as the case system. As I later became aware, he had selected me as a guinea pig, perhaps an expendable guinea pig, for trying out the new method. As a result of the brusque challenge posed by the Dean's question, I ceased lecturing and thenceforth used only the discussion method in that and other courses with which I subsequently was associated.

The going was very tough, particularly for the first couple of years, but Dean Gay was a brave man and an encouraging boss. He took a long chance on a green young instructor who he knew full well was not a genius. But he gave the instructor constant encouragement and loyally backed him up during the very trying period of experimentation.

Both Professor Taussig and Professor Gay were masterly coaches, and it was my good fortune to have had the benefit of their attention. As this experience indicates, moreover, some of the most valuable teaching by men like Taussig and Gay was done outside the classroom. Similarly in a business concern, no matter what training courses are operated, they cannot effectively take the place of coaching by the boss. Coaching can be a major factor in executive achievement.

IV

Keeping Informed

Information is the sustenance of administration. The making of wise decisions is facilitated when the administrator is well informed. And in formulating policies as guides for action by subordinates in the organization, information also is essential.

Following through

An executive's job is not finished, furthermore, when a decision has been made or a policy formulated. He also has a task of following through to ascertain whether his directives are carried out and whether they are producing the results which were anticipated. One of the clichés on business administration which I have encountered most frequently over the years is: "Hire a good man; turn the job over to him; and leave him alone." As its wide repetition implies, the advice in that cliché has certain merits. Of course a good man should be hired for an administrative position. Of course his job should be clearly defined. Of course he should be given a franchise for carrying it out. And, of course, he should be allowed a sufficiently free hand to enable him to take responsibility for the results. Nevertheless, it is also essential that whoever turns the job over to him should be kept informed as to how the work is progressing. An executive who turns a job over to a lieutenant cannot divest himself of responsibility for the lieutenant's handling of the assignment. It is not an acceptable alibi for a chief executive, for example, to report to his board of directors and to the stockholders that a loss has been incurred because one of his lieutenants failed to carry out an assignment. It is a duty of the chief executive to keep himself reasonably informed on the performance of his lieutenants and their subordinates so that deficiencies can be corrected before they have caused serious damage.

The following examples illustrate some of the circumstances which may nullify an executive directive or policy when the follow-through is inadequate.

A large textile manufacturing company adopted a policy of selected distribution for one of its lines which was particularly well suited for that type of marketing. Its new policy was announced and plans adopted for carefully selecting the wholesalers and retailers who were to handle the line. Neither the sales organization nor the customers, however, fully understood the policy and under the stress of competition exceptions to the policy soon began to be made. The plan was so badly manhandled that in less than a year's time it broke down and was discarded, with a substantial loss of good will and prestige to the company. The plan was basically sound, but it was not properly expounded to those who were to carry it out, and the follow-through was wholly inadequate for remedying the lack of understanding by the men on the firing line.

In several companies heavy inventory losses have been incurred when a policy of close inventory control was disregarded by the heads of operating units, who were confident that they could judge the market shrewdly and increase the profits of their departments by accumulating speculative stocks of materials or merchandise. After a company has had such an experience as that, it usually has adopted means for keeping the chief executive and the board of directors adequately informed as to whether their policies on inventory commitments are being carried out, but they have paid dearly for learning the necessity of being kept informed.

Another situation. A company manufacturing machinery had orders on its books in 1947 for its entire potential output for two and one-half years, and it was a policy of the company to treat all its customers alike. Nevertheless the general manager learned accidentally that the sales manager was accepting occasional orders from large customers and personal friends on which he was promising deliveries ahead of other orders already on the books. The sales manager had given lip service to the policy of treating all customers alike but in practice disregarded it when he chose to do so. That was an example of willful disregard of a policy, the sort of thing on which it sometimes is especially difficult to keep informed.

In a factory where items were manufactured which in some sizes weighed 100 to 200 pounds per unit, lifting equipment had been installed for the use of the workmen, so as to protect them against the danger of ruptures or other injuries by heavy lifting. Although a substantial investment had been made in that equipment, a visitor to the plant some time after the installation found that the equipment was not being used. The workmen just did not bother to take the time to put the special equipment in place. There had not been an adequate follow-through after the expenditure for the equipment had been approved. As in so many other instances, it was tacitly assumed that a policy would be carried out once it had been authorized, and the need for following through was neglected.

In some instances a new policy may have unforeseen effects on other policies. In a company manufacturing brushes, for example, a point wage system was installed, to provide incentive to greater production. The company was not faring well, and a couple of years later a new general manager was employed. Among numerous other difficulties, he found that there were frequent complaints on the quality of the company's product and on the punctuality of its deliveries. On investigation he learned that for both foremen and workmen the point wage system placed a high premium on volume of output, with the result that when large orders came along, smaller orders were sidetracked and inspection was lax, thus giving rise to the complaints. When the wage plan was put into effect, an accompanying provision was not made to keep the top executives informed as to its ramifying effects.

Finally, the example may be cited of a baking company formed by the merger of several companies located in different cities. The merged companies were to operate as branches of the new parent company. Among the economies expected to result from the merger were savings by a centralization of purchasing. The branch managers seemed to subscribe in principle to a policy of centralized purchasing, but difficulties soon appeared. Whenever a branch ran short of any raw materials, the manager was permitted, as an emergency measure, to purchase locally in an amount up to $100. It soon appeared that several branches were continually running short of certain items and purchasing them locally; emergency purchasing had become chronic. The right to purchase was regarded by the branch managers as a matter of prestige, and they were loath to give it up. Hence, without adequate control, the policy of central purchasing was being partially nullified.

The foregoing examples are very commonplace and could be multiplied many times over. They illustrate how, in the absence of adequate follow-up, a directive or a policy can be rendered ineffective through lack of understanding, conflicts of interest, the emotions of personal prestige, breaks with tradition, internal politics, and even willful sabotage growing out of envy or other causes. As has been pointed out earlier, instructions or policies announced by an executive do not become effective until they have been accepted by those who are expected to carry them out. In order to achieve results it is a function of an executive to follow through to ascertain whether the instructions and policies have been accepted. And the executive can follow through effectively only when he is properly informed.

Information to facilitate following through, however, is only one of many types of information utilized by executives to aid them in making intelligent plans for action and in performing their other administrative tasks. Let us take a look at this range of executive information.

The range of executive information

In a preceding chapter a question was raised as to what there is left for an executive to do when he has a competent lieutenant in each key position. Well, keeping informed is one of the time-consuming tasks of an executive. In fact the range of information in which an executive potentially is interested is so wide that he needs must pick and choose from the abundant supply available. The following are some of the items included in the range of information with which an executive is concerned; other items will be pointed out from time to time in later chapters.

First come the periodic accounting and statistical reports, in such detail and with such summaries as each executive may determine to be best suited to his own needs. The accounting and statistical reports are a major item in the executive information service, but their nature is so well known that it does not seem necessary to go into detail on that subject here.

In addition to the regular accounting and statistical reports received by a chief executive, he typically also receives various special reports on a wide variety of subjects, such as a proposal for building an addition to a plant or for scrapping an obsolete plant, the purchase of a new type of equipment, the potential market for a new product, the raw material situation, the company's prospective financial needs, and many other topics, varying according to the current requirements and problems of the business.

The chief executive nowadays also is likely to receive periodic reports on general business conditions, which in some companies are supplemented by comparative analyses of the company's own operations and outlook. This is a relatively new development in industry. Up until the First World War the ups and downs of business activity usually were explained in political terms. Hard times then were commonly attributed to the Democrats and prosperity credited to the Republicans, a theory which obviously could be applied with little intellectual effort. In earlier years a few attempts had been made to interpret business fluctuations in terms of sun spots or pig-iron prices, but no comprehensive economic analyses had been undertaken. Shortly before the First World War several services were established for forecasting business conditions, but the major change came after 1918, when such well-known economists as Wesley C. Mitchell, Warren M. Persons, and Charles J. Bullock took the lead in the economic analysis of business conditions. They have been followed by many other able analysts.

The analysts of the 1920's generally did not foresee the collapse which started in 1929, but that failure only led to more searching analyses. Today the scientific analysis of business conditions is by no means perfected, but substantial progress has been made and a new point of view widely established among business executives. It is not reasonable to expect that periods of hard times will never occur again, but the change in point of view toward the causes of business fluctuations seems to me to be highly significant.

After the end of the Second World War, for example, there was not a repetition of some of the excesses which had led to the slump in 1920–21. If a lesson had not been learned from the earlier experience, a far more severe reaction probably would have occurred in the late 1940's.[4] More and more attention, furthermore, is now being given to means of preventing or at least mitigating the severity of business depressions. While an individual corporation alone cannot do much to prevent a depression, an awareness of the problem and the adoption of sound policies by numerous corporations, each acting intelligently with reference to its own problems, can contribute substantially, I believe, to an alleviation of the severity of business fluctuations. At all events, general business conditions now constitute one of the topics on which a progressive executive leader seeks to keep himself informed.

The range of information with which an executive is concerned includes not only the formal accounting and statistical reports, various special reports, and data on business conditions, but also informal information received from his lieutenants in the course of his discussions with them, from others in the organization with whom he comes in contact, from customers, and from miscellaneous sources. How much information he obtains from such sources depends in part upon how good a listener he is, how shrewdly he senses leads

[4] Whether this lesson has been fully learned remains to be seen. Toward the end of 1950 it appeared that the current inflationary procedures of the federal government, of some state governments, of certain labor groups, and of some business concerns, together with hoarding by consumers, might be tending to create the sort of feverish situation from which in years gone by business slumps have eventuated. Then came the necessary preparations for large-scale defense mobilization which lessened the likelihood of any immediate slump in economic activity but which did not provide assurance that a slump might not occur at some later date.

or clues, and how penetratingly he follows up those leads or clues with pertinent questions.

The chief executive of one large company has a motto framed on the wall behind his desk:

> A wise old owl sat on an oak,
> The more he saw the less he spoke;
> The less he spoke the more he heard;
> Why aren't we like that wise old bird?

The primary purpose of having that motto displayed so prominently, I assume, is to discourage garrulous callers. Nevertheless the executive himself is a good listener and usually follows the precept of the motto.

Listening is an art. The good listener can judge whether a person has something worth while to say and help him to say it, if need be, by asking encouraging questions. The good listener also can judge when he has heard all the significant information likely to be obtained from that source.

A good listener also is a shrewd observer. He knows that in some instances what a person is saying is of less significance than the manner in which he says it. If a person comes into an executive's office "to get something off his chest," the fact that he "has something on his chest" is likely to be more significant than the gripe which he voices. It probably indicates some smoldering emotion, the cause of which may be quite revealing if it can be uncovered.

A business executive who is an adept at listening thus utilizes that device not only as a means of procuring factual information about the operation of the business but for highly significant supplementary purposes as well. He thereby learns of situations charged with emotion, for which he well may seek to find some nonexplosive vent. From what he hears while listening he also may spot clues as to conditions which call for further careful investigation. He thus may uncover incipient problems, for example, before they become troublesome. Of not the least importance, finally, is the opportunity which listening provides for making an appraisal of people in the organization.

An executive who is a good listener coaches his lieutenants also to be good listeners and to report to him frankly what they learn, even though it may have disagreeable or annoying implications. The chief executive of an enterprise of any size cannot possibly confer personally at frequent intervals with all the superintendents, foremen, salesmen, and employees. Much of the information which he needs regarding their problems and their attitudes must be funneled up to him through the organization, and it easily can become distorted or dammed up on the way or smothered at the source.

There is a natural tendency for subordinates to report information which will be to their credit and information which they think that the boss will like to hear. There is also a tendency for them to omit or suppress other information. They may hope to curry favor, or they may feel that the security of their jobs is at stake. The overcoming of such tendencies is one of the major tasks of an executive who would be well informed.

Good listening, especially by the boss, is essential to good teamwork. Teamwork connotes membership on a team, where there is both give and take. Each member of a management team normally wants to feel that he is respected and that at least some of his ideas will be deemed worthy of being heard. Unless this point of view is recognized by the leader, his effectiveness is impaired, as in the following situation. A couple of years ago the managers of the branches of a New York department store were called to New York for an all-day conference on certain problems of personnel management. During the day they were told how those problems were handled in the big store, and it was indicated to them that they were expected to adopt similar methods in the branches of which they were in charge. None of the branch managers were asked to report on their experience or to express any views on the applicability of the big store's methods to their particular situations. At least some of the branch managers felt after the conference that they had been treated arrogantly, and that feeling arose chiefly from the fact that they had not been permitted to express any views of their own. They had not been listened to. Consequently, they did not accept their instructions with enthusiasm.

One of the lessons which I had driven home to me most forcibly during my service with the War Industries Board in Washington in the First World War was the importance of granting interested parties a chance to be heard before final action was taken. I found that most men were not nearly so concerned over the particular action taken as they were over having a chance to express their views before a final decision was reached. They usually would accept the decision with good grace, even when not in accord with their personal interests, provided the decision was not arbitrarily rammed down their throats. I have observed that the same attitude is prevalent in business operations, and it certainly obtains in an academic institution.

As the foregoing somewhat rambling observations indicate, the range of information with which a business executive is concerned is wide and diverse. It varies, at least in emphasis, from company to company and in the degree to which different types of information are formalized. As has been indicated, furthermore, there has been a notable increase in recent years in the quantity of information available, and that increase in supply seems to have whetted the executive appetite for still more facts. This is a subject which touches upon some of my tenderest personal experiences.

When I was a graduate student in economics, over forty years ago, I accepted the implications in the textbooks that every businessman knew his costs accurately and was guided by them. Indeed on any other premise much of the theorizing would have had little significance. Then I began to become acquainted with some of the realities of business life.

My first experience was with the cotton manufacturing industry, where I was gathering material for a doctoral thesis. I did a good deal of library work, but both Professor Taussig and Professor Gay urged me to get out into the field and obtain some information at first hand. In the course of my field work I encountered a number of situations which did not seem to jibe with the textbook assumptions, but the real significance of that early experience did not become apparent to me until some years later.

In the summer of 1913, after I had become an instructor in the newly established Harvard Business School, I participated in the pioneer research work which had been started two years earlier for a study of the cost of doing business in retail shoe stores. At that time many shoe retailers, we found, did not have accurate records and did not know their costs. Sometimes they would not admit it. The president of a large department store in New York, for example, vehemently refused to give up his confidential information — what he called "the guts of his business." Some years later I learned that his figures were so incomplete that he had been ashamed to admit it to the research representative. This was probably the most dramatic of several such experiences.

During the next few years I participated in similar studies in several other retail and wholesale trades, in every one of which we found numerous instances of a lack of knowledge of costs and other operating data which the textbooks implied every businessman had at his fingertips. I was becoming disillusioned.

For twenty-one months in 1917–18 I was in Washington as executive secretary of the Commercial Economy Board which later became the Conservation Division of the War Industries Board. When Armistice Day came we had conservation programs in force or ready to be issued for 261 industries. Again, while these programs were being developed, I had discovered many surprising instances of companies or whole industries which did not have command of all the available facts regarding their operations.

In December 1920, after I had returned to the Business School, we began the collection of cases through our research organization. The cases, collected at first hand in the field, were to be used for teaching purposes. These clinical studies revealed still other instances of incomplete information.

Then in 1926 came an experience which completed my disillusionment. At that time I was employed as a consultant on marketing problems by a large textile company. One evening while engaged in a discussion with several junior executives of the company, I suggested that we undertake to get some facts on the problem under consideration. That suggestion was greeted with remarks and sly winks which indicated that my habitual practice of seeking facts was a sufficiently novel approach to cause amusement to those executives. What I had been doing naïvely as a matter of course was almost revolutionary to them.

A few years later I was serving as consultant to another large company in a different industry. After I had been on the job about a year, I had occasion to ask the executive vice president about a certain problem. He looked up at me with a grin and said: "This time we have applied Dr. Copeland's formula. We have been getting some facts together on this problem."

I still frequently encounter business situations where there is a remediable dearth of pertinent data. Nevertheless over the last forty years I have observed a growing tendency for business executives to take a more analytical approach to their problems and to seek to become better informed. The range of executive information has been widening.

This widening of the range of executive information has been accompanied by major improvements in the techniques of obtaining, analyzing, and presenting information. In accounting and business statistics, for example, substantial changes in techniques have taken place. In the area of human relations, pioneering research by Mayo, Roethlisberger, and their associates has opened up significant new technical methods of obtaining basic data. And in various other areas new and improved methods of securing pertinent information have been developed. None of these methods are yet perfect, however. Great opportunities undoubtedly still exist for further worth-while development of executive information.

Combating remoteness

As a corporation increases in size, the top executives tend to become more and more remote from the foremen, the workers in the plant, the salesmen, the customers, and, if the stock is widely owned, from the stockholders. The need for information is not lessened, but the difficulties of securing it become increasingly greater.

The head of a machine manufacturing company of modest volume, located in a small New England city, recently stated: "I know the men in our shop by name. I see them at church and at town functions. I know their families. We are all part of the same community." In a business thus situated there is easy communication and a ready opportunity for mutual understanding, and there are thousands of business concerns in the United States where such conditions do obtain.

As a result of the economies of mass production and other large-scale operations, however, there are many other industries in which it is not possible for the executives to maintain such intimate acquaintanceship with employees, or with customers, or with stockholders, or with the local public. The larger the corporation, the more tiers in the administrative hierarchy and the more remote the top executives become from the rank and file of the workers and from those other groups which in a broad sense constitute essential parts of the enterprise. One of the prices which we have to pay for enjoying the economies of large-scale operations is the risk of executive remoteness.

Executive remoteness can occur, of course, in a small business enterprise or even in an educational institution. Unapproachable executives are remote and usually are not well informed, whatever the type or size of the undertaking. But the problem takes on special significance in the case of large business enterprises.

In numerous companies physical remoteness of the top executives from at least some of the operating units is unavoidable. When a company is operating several plants, for example, headquarters are located either at one of the plants or in a large city such as New York or Chicago. In such companies, the choice of the location of headquarters is governed by numerous factors, including accessibility, market relationships, financial connections, and even perhaps by the personal preference of an executive or his wife. Irrespective of the considerations which determine the location of the headquarters of such companies, physical remoteness of the top executives from at least some of the operating units does result, and thereby the task of the executives of keeping themselves informed is further complicated.

"Absentee management" is a term often applied to a situation in which the headquarters of a company are separated from the operating units. That phrase "absentee management," however, usually implies not only a physical remoteness of the executives but a feeling on the part of the natives that the outside executives do not have a sympathetic understanding of local working conditions or that they are indifferent to local community relationships. Such feelings may be quite unwarranted, but when they do exist they indicate that the executives have not been able to keep themselves fully informed or, if informed, that they have failed to utilize that information effectively.

In a company operating several plants, the lack of mutual understanding between top management, the supervisory force, and the workers is well illustrated in a recent report[5] by three members of the research staff of the Harvard Business School. The company's headquarters were located in New York City, and the plants were located between 100 and 500 miles from New York. It appeared from the intimate first-hand observations of these research men in one of the plants that the top executives had not made their point of view and their policies fully clear to the supervisory force and the workers in the plant. It also was apparent that the top executives did not have a comprehensive, sympathetic understanding of the problems and the attitudes of the foremen and the workers. That is a very commonplace situation in industry. It emanates from executive remoteness or at least is aggravated by that remoteness. Such conditions as that, furthermore, are the inherent source of some of the strife in industry and a prolific cause of public animosity toward business.

In the early 1930's a new president was elected for a large textile company operating over a dozen mills. His office was located in New York City where sales activities naturally were

[5] David N. Ulrich, Donald R. Booz, and Paul R. Lawrence, *Management Behavior and Foreman Attitude: A Case Study* (Boston: Division of Research, Harvard Business School, 1950).

focused. Two years after the new president had been installed, he was criticized by certain minority stockholding interests for never having visited several of the mills. That criticism presumably emanated from some of the disgruntled members of the operating staffs of the mills who were dissatisfied with some of the new policies introduced by the president. Even though he may have kept himself adequately informed on many aspects of the operations of the mills, he had left himself open to attacks on the ground of "absentee management." Even though his technical information may have been adequate, he did not have a full understanding of the human problems involved in operating the mills.

The problems of remoteness connoted by the phrase "absentee management" still constitute a major challenge for executive leadership in numerous corporations. How can a top executive learn of the attitudes and reactions of employees and supervisory force, particularly in dispersed operating units? How can he keep himself properly informed of the relations between the operating units and the people in the communities where they are located? Those are questions not easily answered, but satisfactory answers are essential in order to provide a basis for the effective handling of employee relations and public relations.

To turn to another aspect of the broad problem of remoteness, the case of a large American department store can be cited as an example of executive remoteness from customers. In 1947 a customer purchased several pieces of rather expensive furniture at the store. When delivery was made, the customer found that the merchandise delivered was not what had been ordered. The store was notified. And after some delay the customer received a notice that "the store does not exchange furniture." The customer explained that he was not seeking to exchange furniture but merely to obtain the furniture which he had bought. This procedure was repeated over and over again for several months, until in desperation the customer went to an executive high enough in the organization to comprehend the simple facts in the case.

The one isolated experience cited above would have limited significance were it not for the fact that almost every family which is a regular customer of that store has had analogous experiences with errors in filling orders, or with mistakes in the monthly bills, or with other annoying deficiencies in service to customers. Presumably the top executives of that company are not aware of how widespread the customer irritation is. They probably are too remote from the customers and too inadequately informed on the deficiencies in the relations of the store to its customers to sense the precariousness of their position. There are other department stores in the country, however, as large or larger than the one referred to above which have developed far happier relations with their customers. The executives of the stores with good customer relations keep themselves sufficiently well informed to enable them to take corrective steps promptly whenever any maladjustment in their service to customers begins to appear.

Little things give rise to some of the major problems in business administration, and yet the little things commonly are the most difficult to unearth. Avoiding the loss of customers is an objective of most businesses, but the reasons why a particular customer discontinues his patronage is sometimes not easy of ascertainment. Some years ago the president of a large wholesale hardware company in St. Louis, for example, had occasion to be in a certain town in Texas. While there for other purposes, he availed himself of the opportunity to call on a retailer who formerly had been a good customer but who had completely stopped buying from that firm. The wholesale company had been unable to obtain any satisfactory explanation from its salesman or from the customer for the estrangement. When the president entered the store, the retailer gave him a thoroughly chilly reception and for some minutes thereafter would vouchsafe no explanation for his discontinuance of patronage. Finally the retailer blurted out, with considerable profanity, that some months before, shortly after he had had a new hardwood floor laid in his store, the wholesaler's salesman had spat tobacco juice on that new floor and he, the retailer, had vowed that he would never buy another dime's worth of merchandise from the firm by which that salesman was employed. Perhaps the chief significance of this episode is the fact that the president of the wholesale company was informed as to the loss of individual customers and that he personally was concerned to find out, when he could, the reasons for each defection.

Combating remoteness from the various elements in the social group which go to make up a business enterprise and support its activities is one of the tasks of an executive leader. In order to combat remoteness, the executive first must be aware of the problem. Then in the selection of his lieutenants and their subordinates an opportunity is afforded for laying the groundwork to combat remoteness by choosing persons who are good teamworkers and who will be coöperative in keeping the executive informed. The instructions given to the lieutenants and the coaching which they receive also can aid in dealing with the problems of remoteness. At the same time there is need for providing for an upflow of information which will reveal to the executive the attitudes, motivations, and reactions of the other participants in the enterprise. The stimulation of this upflow and the interpretation of the information constitute one of the least developed phases of business administration. The problem is receiving increasing attention in many corporations, and significant new developments are likely to take place in the not distant future.

Action anyway

The purpose of an executive in keeping himself informed is to make possible intelligent and timely action. Mere facts, however, seldom provide automatic answers to the problems which come up for executive decision. Administration involves far more than the finding of ready-made answers. A shoe retailer some years ago, for example, asked one of our research assistants about a new stock-keeping system. He remarked that he had tried five different systems and that "none of them were any damn good"—they had not improved the rate of stock turn in his store. He was looking for a "system" which would work without effort on his part. That attitude is a rather common one, but administration cannot be made effortless.

Facts are useful in administration, but they are only the starting point. They must be analyzed, interpreted, and weighed. The members of an executive's staff may aid him in the analysis and interpretation of the facts, but ultimately the responsibility for the intelligent use of the information rests on him.

Unless an executive is willing to face the facts squarely and honestly, furthermore, the information is useless. Facing the facts sometimes is painful, since it may involve acknowledgment of having made a mistake. The executives of one company with whose affairs I had occasion to become familiar were seeking a solution to the high operating costs in their sales branches. After considerable digging the facts showed that much of the trouble arose in one branch, and eventually it appeared that conditions were inherently unfavorable to the operation of a sales branch in that region. A mistake had been made in opening the branch, but even when that conclusion was pointed out, with ample substantiation, the executives were reluctant to admit their mistake. They were still hopeful that someone could pull a rabbit out of a hat which would make an unsound operation into a healthy one.

In another instance, the president of a shoe manufacturing company, which had tried a variety of marketing expedients, was very much annoyed at a research report that cast doubts upon the opportunities for successful operation by a manufacturing company of leased departments in retail stores. It happened that his latest experiment, after several others had failed, was with leased departments, and he was not prepared to face the possibility that he had made another mistake. Facts can be painful, and a willingness to face facts even when they are painful is a real test of executive competency.

In a preceding section of this chapter, the range of executive information has been reviewed. It is now necessary, it seems to me, to recognize that while the range of information available to many an executive is so wide that at times he seems to be in danger of being swamped by it, nevertheless it also is true that many decisions by practically every executive have to be made with a dearth of factual information. Such situations undoubtedly will continue to exist.

Some facts are so elusive that it is practically impossible to put one's finger on them. This is particularly true in that large area of administration which involves dealings with human beings — employees of many ranks, customers, stockholders, public officials, and the public at large. The human motivations and the human emotions involved in many such situations are particularly elusive factors.

Still another major reason for the dearth of facts in numerous situations is the continual changes which are taking place. Conditions change and new developments occur. But decisions often have to be made before the new developments have had time to produce recorded results. In 1949–50, for example, television was expanding rapidly. Practically every company using radio in a large way for advertising had to decide then whether to add television to its advertising program or to substitute television for radio advertising. Those decisions had to be made with little information as to the effectiveness of television as an advertising medium.

However much information a business executive has at his disposal, it is inevitable that many of his decisions will have to be made with incomplete facts. That is inherent in the nature of the executive's job in a dynamic world. He should keep himself as well informed as possible, but in order to achieve results he must have the courage as well as the judgment to make decisions when need be without many facts. This is one of the heavy burdens of executive responsibility.

V

Keeping the Wheels Turning

In business administration, as in so many other human activities, humdrum duties bulk large. The task of keeping the wheels turning, day in and day out, has little glamour. The regular performance of that task is assumed as a matter of course by experienced executives, but it is not easily dramatized or readily systematized into convenient pigeonholes. It is just plain, ordinary, commonplace, everyday work.

The daily drive

About the best definition of administration I know is that it is "just one damn thing after another." I do not recall where that definition orginated, but it reveals heartfelt understanding of the work of an executive. In my own modest administrative job, I often go to work in the morning with a light schedule in prospect, but about the time the mail arrives numerous other problems begin to appear, presented personally, or over the telehone, or by memorandum. Thus it goes, hammer and tongs, all day. At night I go home with ample realization that it has been a busy period even though there may be some difficulty in pointing to specific things accomplished. In that respect administration has much in common with teaching. As a teacher I often found it difficult to feel assured that the students had learned much of anything on any particular day. At the end of the term, however, many of them usually seemed to have acquired some training, enough in fact to encourage the teacher to try it again when the next batch of students came along. So in business administration it is the cumulative effect of the day-by-day detailed operations which pays off. By keeping the wheels turning, results are produced.

The chief executive is both a cause and a victim of the daily drive. He is a cause since he is responsible for putting on the pressure to get things done. He is a victim, since the more pressure he applies to others, the heavier the recoil on him.

The burden of the daily drive is intensified for the executive because normally only the toughest problems come to him — the ones that are referred to him by the board of directors and the ones which his lieutenants do not feel authorized or qualified to decide. Some of these problems are of the sort where there is a dearth of information. If a decision has to be made before adequate information can be gathered, it is likely to be the top executive who is asked to take the responsibility of making that decision. On some of the tough questions the executive may seek the counsel and advice of the directors, but he has to prepare himself in advance for such discussions.

The day-to-day task of keeping the wheels turning also requires the executive to be shifting his attention continually from production to sales, to finance, to merchandising, to personnel, to public relations, and so on in an interminable but ever varying sequence. To be sure, there is likely to be greater emphasis on one class of problems at certain times, as for example on production during the war years or on marketing when productive capacity tends to outrun demand, but the whole gamut is there, and the executive has to be ready to shift from one category of problems to another without notice.

When we ultimately discover the basic tests of executive ability, I expect that the capacity to make quick mental switches will rank high on the list. From my own limited observations, I judge such capacity to be rare. A great many people — a large majority, I judge — do not have either the interest or the capacity to acquire the knack of making quick mental switches in the consideration of substantial problems. The mental wear and tear of continually making such switches is heavy. These circumstances, I believe, constitute one of the major reasons why there is always a dearth of highly competent executive talent.

To underscore the difficulty which so many men have in making frequent and rapid mental switches, perhaps it will not be amiss for me to refer to some experiences on another scale. Early in my research work in the field of marketing, I found that when a company was catering to two different markets, such as the consumer market and the industrial market, for example, better results typically were secured by segregating the sales force into two groups, one for each type of market. It appeared that ordinarily a salesman could not be continually shifting back and forth between different types of buyers without having his effectiveness materially impaired. The buying habits and the buying motives of the two types of buyers were so different as to involve difficult mental shifts by the salesmen striving to cater to both. In several other types of situations, segregation of the sales force seemed to be more effective when the volume of sales was large enough to permit it. Another way of stating the same conclusion would be to say that if the salesmen are expected to seek the patronage of two or more types of customers, men of substantially higher mental capacity will have to be hired than when each salesman concentrates on a single class of buyers.

My other example centers around an experience which occurred in November 1921, but which could have occurred in 1951. There are several versions of this story, told somewhat differently by various people concerned, but all involving the same fundamental point. When I returned to my office from class one forenoon, I found the secretary of a large company which manufactured heating equipment waiting for me. He had talked to Dean Donham, and the Dean had referred him to me. As he told it later, he explained the company's problem to me at length, only to have me observe finally that his business was a good deal like the jewelry business. As he repeated the story he reported that he was somewhat flabbergasted at that remark and that he wondered "why in hell the dean had sent him over to talk to that damn fool professor." He had no interest in the jewelry business. He was there to talk about the marketing of heating equipment.

Our subsequent discussion, however, established the validity of the analogy. A couple of years before, we had undertaken in our research program to study the cost of doing business in retail jewelry stores. When that study was begun, I had expected that it would be easier to get data from retail jewelers than it had been from shoe retailers, retail grocers, hardware retailers, and retail druggists. But the jewelers proved to be the toughest nut we had tried to crack. As I explained to my visitor, I had just discovered the reason for that unexpected toughness. Many retail jewelers had started business as watch repairers, and they were more interested in looking at the inside of a watch through their eye glass than they were in the display and sale of merchandise in their show cases. They had an artisan's, not a merchant's, point of view, and most of them could not be both good artisans and good merchants. They could not switch readily back and forth between merchandising and repairing, and some of them seemed almost to resent having their repair work interrupted by a merchandise customer.

The point to the analogy was that this company manufacturing heating equipment was seeking distribution through retail plumbing establishments. The company needed merchants to retail its wares. But the plumber, like the jeweler, was primarily an artisan. Hence the company was struggling to secure distribution through artisans who were not merchants, and it looked like an almost hopeless task to find dealers who were both artisans and merchants. As a recent purchaser of plumbing materials, I judge that that basic problem has not yet been mastered.

To return from this digression, the executive must deal with production, marketing, finance, personnel, and numerous problems every day, continually shifting from one to another. The task of making those shifts is an exacting one.

Despite all the pressures to which an executive is subject in day-to-day operations, furthermore, he can keep the wheels turning more effectively if he organizes his work so that he is accessible for consultation by his lieutenants on short notice. Ready accessibility and promptness in the making of decisions help materially to expedite operations. When a lieutenant normally can gain a prompt hearing from the boss, the lieutenant's enthusiasm is intensified and that enthusiasm is reflected in the results attained. So far as my own observations go, it is a matter of administrative habit whether an executive is prompt or dilatory in becoming accessible to his lieutenants. In the end it takes no more time and involves less mental wear and tear to do things promptly.

I once had a colleague, a man of very high ideals and great integrity, who always was so busy that we usually had to wait one to two months to get him to read a manuscript, for example, which most of our other associates would read within a few days or a week. He always was a long way behind on his commitments, but so far as I could observe he never accomplished more, perhaps less, than our prompt colleagues. A matter of habit.

Postscript: The foregoing shoe may fit more than one academic foot.

Getting things done

In order to achieve results, an executive at times must become a driver. Results are achieved not merely by precept, inspiration, and example; under some conditions in every organization leadership calls for forceful driving. Occasions arise with sufficient frequency to be significant when patient tolerance no longer suffices, when the executive has to pound the desk, at least figuratively speaking, and decree emphatically that certain things must be done and done by a stipulated time.

On the wall of our office in Washington during the First World War, we had a motto which we obtained from the Navy. It read: "It can't be done, but here it is." That motto to me epitomizes one major aspect of an executive's job, the accomplishing of things which faint hearts and timid souls declare to be impossible.

Although the chief executive officer of an organization typically has the responsibility for providing the drive as well as the perspective, a division of that responsibility in some instances has been found to be effective. Alex Legge, executive vice president of the War Industries Board in the First World War, for example, was the driver. Mr. Baruch, suave, genial, keen-minded, inspirational, and canny, maintained relations with the White House, Congress, and various high dignitaries. He also was firm, levelheaded, and farsighted, "the Chief" to whom everyone in the organization was extremely loyal. It is no disparagement of "the Chief," however, to point out that Alex Legge contributed far more to the successful operation of the War Industries Board than ever has been recognized publicly. In fact, the recognition of Alex Legge's contribution is another tribute to the great wisdom of "the Chief" in selecting such a capable man to perform an essential task.

Alex Legge, on leave of absence from the general managership of the International Harvester Company, was over six feet tall, rawboned, and earthy, with a cowboy's vocabulary. He had quick insight, level judgment, and a dry wit. Day after day he dealt with the men who were working on requirements for the armed forces, priorities, conservation, and numerous other activities. He handled many of the detailed top administrative problems. Within the organization we all knew him as the friendly but forceful executive who succeeded in getting things done. He and "the Chief" constituted a highly effective administrative pair.

In industry administrative pairs of that type also are found. In the case of one large, well-known corporation, the chairman of the board of directors and the president for many years worked together as such a pair. The chairman gave especial attention to questions of long-run policy and to public relations in addition to serving as the head of an active board of directors. The president forcefully directed operations. It was his task to get things done and he did get them done. The two men had a high regard for each other's ability and jointly participated in the consideration of major problems. While each had a special set of functions to perform, they operated effectively to achieve both long-range objectives and immediate results.

In still another case, of a much smaller company, the president and chief owner is an exuberant, imaginative promoter. Soon after he acquired control of the company he employed another man as general manager, who is calm, analytical, levelheaded, and systematic in his procedure. He maintains the steady pressure to get things done and keeps the wheels turning day after day. Both are drivers in one sense, but they supplement each other to a marked degree. This is another example of an administrative pair.

Still another type of organizational setup to expedite administration is illustrated by the following experience. This is a large company. At one time, even after it had reached a stage where it was producing a wide variety of products and selling them to diverse markets, the company had a functional administrative setup, with a general sales manager in charge of all sales divisions and a general production manager in charge of all manufacturing activities. This resulted in what one of my business acquaintances has called a "hairpin curve" type of organization, as illustrated in Chart I, simplified by omission of staff officers and others who were not primarily concerned with the problem to which attention is directed here.

Although many of the products were made from the same raw materials, the A products were manufactured in one plant, the B products in another plant, and so on. On the sales side, there were fairly distinct markets for each group of products, without substantial overlapping. Under the setup in Chart I, which had its antecedents in the much simpler operations of an earlier period, the management of sales and the management of production were functionalized, with all the alleged advantages of such functionalization. In operation, however, that setup was cumbersome. On many questions the production manager and the sales manager of D products, for instance, could informally short-circuit the organization chart by settling matters by mutual agreement. But whenever a question arose which they could not settle, the only court of appeal was the president, with the issue routed through the

Chart I

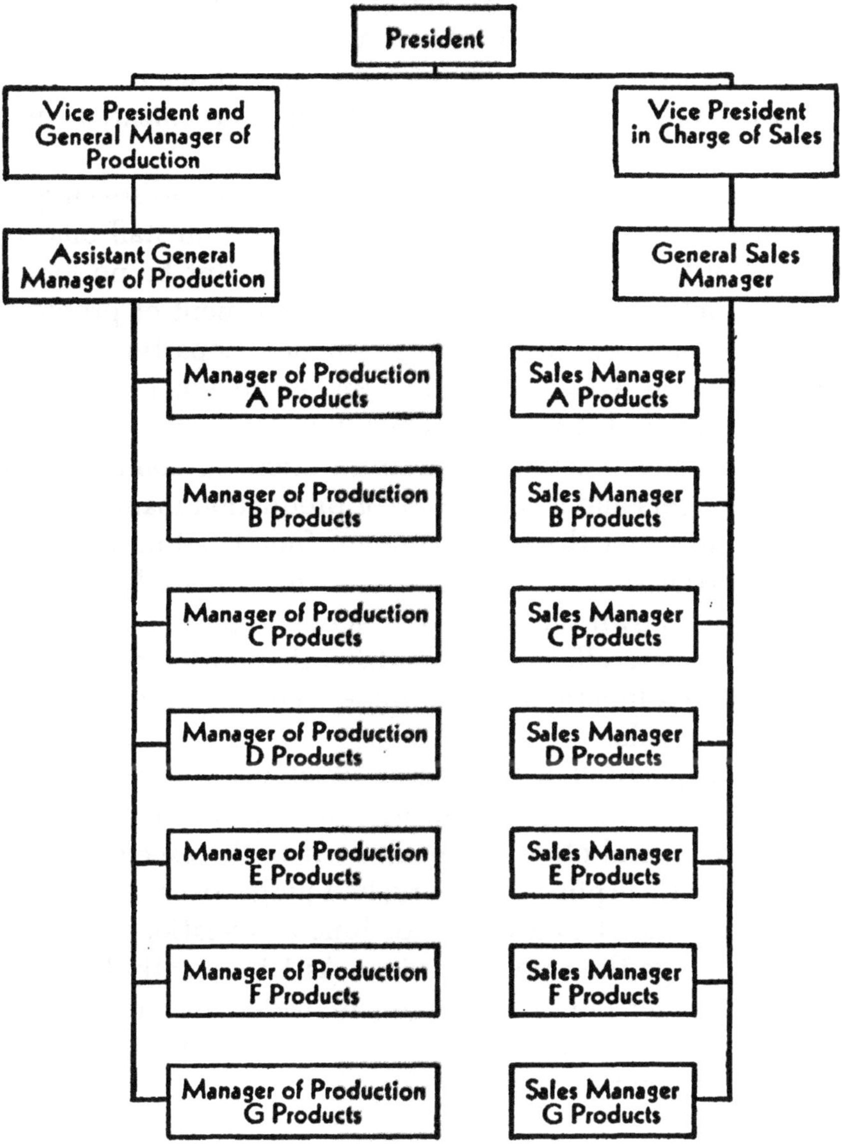
President
Vice President and General Manager of Production
Vice President in Charge of Sales
Assistant General Manager of Production
General Sales Manager
Manager of Production A Products
Sales Manager A Products
Manager of Production B Products
Sales Manager B Products
Manager of Production C Products
Sales Manager C Products
Manager of Production D Products
Sales Manager D Products
Manager of Production E Products
Sales Manager E Products
Manager of Production F Products
Sales Manager F Products
Manager of Production G Products
Sales Manager G Products

assistant general manager of production and the vice president and general manager of production on the one side and the general sales manager and vice president in charge of sales on the other side. That was a long, slow route of settlement. The use of that setup tended to slow down rather than expedite operations. Consequently the organization was changed, as indicated in Chart II.

Under the new organization the president had seven general managers reporting to him, besides certain staff officers, instead of two functional vice presidents. But he no longer was the only court of appeal for the settlement of problems involving only the sales and production departments of a single division. This type of divisional setup, where both production and market for each product or group of products are largely distinct, facilitates administration. A committee of sales managers and a committee of production managers can function to foster the interchange of functional information. But the provision of a general manager for each division, each with its own sales and production departments, makes possible a more effective daily drive than ordinarily can be attained by a functional setup under such conditions of production and sale.

I am acquainted with several situations where the divisional general manager setup has effectively been adopted. There are several other companies where the executives still cling to their hairpin curves, largely, I judge, because they are so firmly wedded to a theory of functionalization that they cannot change their point of view. As I frequently have occasion to point out, I long ago discovered that one of the hardest tasks to be encountered anywhere is to get a man to change his point of view.

The job of getting things done, we may as well recognize, is sometimes a painful one, so let us turn now to a few of the painful aspects of administration.

Chart II

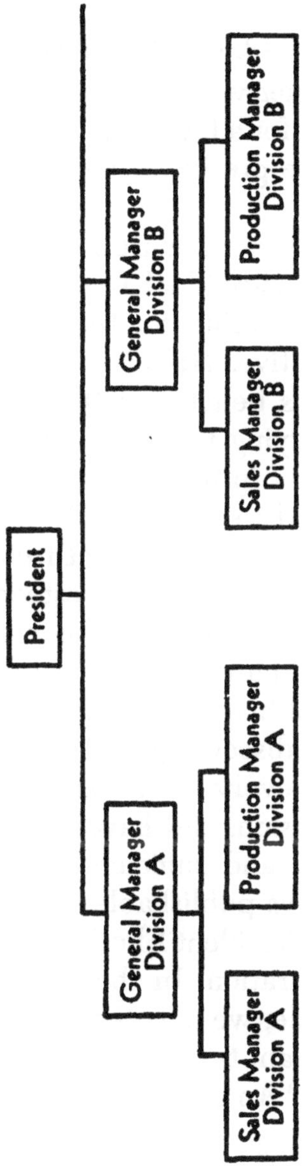

(Seven divisions in all)

Painful tasks

Of the late President Eliot it is stated by his biographer: "To a questioner who asked him, after he had been at the head of Harvard for a few years, to name the quality most essential to a college president, he answered, 'The capacity to inflict pain.'"[1]

President Eliot was not a martinet. Quite the contrary. He was a champion of individual freedom. But he also had a high sense of responsibility for the institution of which he was the chief executive. His biographer also stated that it was President Eliot's belief that the president "must never be charged with playing favorites; he must not be tempted by friendship to falter in the service of the institution whose welfare was confided to his care. He must be ready to say NO as often as YES, and to disappoint frequently. He must be explicit when it hurt another's self-esteem to state the exact truth, lest he should leave room for misunderstanding. He tried so hard to avoid arousing hopes which it might not be possible to fulfill that his candor was disconcerting and sometimes unnecessarily discouraging. He knew that it must fall to his lot to enforce every harsh decision that might have to be made. Hard decisions did have to be enforced now and then, and the good and sufficient reasons which dictated them were not always publishable."[2]

In large measure President Eliot's views also are applicable to business administration. In the study of directors which Mr. Towl and I made, we devoted a chapter to a consideration of some unpleasant tasks which have to be performed by a board of directors.[3] An executive, as indicated by the refer-

[1] Henry James, *Charles W. Eliot* (Boston: Houghton Mifflin, 1930), I, 309–310.

[2] *Ibid.*, p. 309.

[3] Melvin T. Copeland and Andrew R. Towl, *The Board of Directors and Business Management* (Boston: Division of Research, Harvard Business School, 1947).

ence to President Eliot's experience, also has unpleasant duties to perform.

An unpleasant executive task of most frequent occurrence in business is the necessity of informing some member of the organization that his services no longer are needed. If the cause for firing is some overt immorality or breach of faith, the necessity for action is readily apparent. It is annoying to have to deal with such cases, but they can be disposed of without great pain.

Oftentimes, however, the man who has to be fired is personally a very likable chap, with no bad habits, who just does not measure up to his responsibilities. His deficiencies, moreover, may be of a sort which he himself cannot understand. Indeed if he could understand them perhaps he could correct them. The causes which produce such cases are of great variety — inherent limitations on ability, physical health, mental health, moral stamina, family life, and many others.

With some of these cases it is very painful to deal. Yet for the good of the enterprise, action must be taken. Any executive who knowingly is tolerant of second-rate performance in his organization is not likely to have a first-rate enterprise, at least not for long.

Delay in dealing with such cases seldom makes the task less painful, and delay may make matters worse. I have seldom observed any gratitude on the part of the man himself for delay in firing him, provided he has had a fair chance to prove his capacity. Sometimes there is an analogy with the experience of a wholesale jeweler in granting credit to a customer. The retailer bought merchandise at first on the usual thirty-day credit terms. Presently he could not pay his bills on time so he gave the wholesaler a ninety-day note. Every three months thereafter the note was renewed, and usually increased since he continued to have difficulty in financing new purchases. Finally, after three years, the debt was becoming so large and the likelihood of repayment so slim that the wholesaler felt impelled to notify the retailer that his note would not be renewed and that he would be granted no further credit. Whereupon the retailer wrote to the wholesaler a bitter letter, in which he damned the wholesaler for having granted him credit in the first place. "It is all your fault," he wrote, "for having let me get into this predicament." I have noted similar emotional reactions in numerous other cases of frustration and disappointment.

The performance of certain unpleasant tasks inevitably falls upon the shoulders of the chief executive. Despite care in the selection of members of the staff and despite efforts to develop their competency, occasions will arise when dismissals have to be made. Cutbacks in operations and changes in plans also sometimes necessitate reductions in administrative personnel or shifts in assignments. In some instances retirement of an aging member of the organization causes grief. Even a promotion also may have its painful aspects, the disappointment of those who are passed over. Even though the executive strives to handle each case with consideration and fairness, these situations are unpleasant to deal with.

These tasks cannot be delegated by the executive to someone else without loss of prestige for the executive himself. Although in each particular case regret, sympathy, and even misunderstanding are likely to arise in certain quarters, particularly in those cases in which the reasons for the action cannot be stated without causing unwarranted harm, nevertheless the members of an organization are likely to be aware that such action must be taken from time to time, and they do not really respect an executive who flinches from squarely meeting such situations. The executive who evades the making of necessary but unpleasant decisions cannot preserve his leadership. The "good fellow" who strives to please everybody usually ends up by pleasing nobody.

The making of unpopular and unwelcome decisions may give the impression that an executive is "hard boiled." It has been remarked, however, that the way to become hard boiled is to stay in hot water long enough, an experience not uncommon for executives. Whatever the impression may be, the capacity to say "no" at the right time often helps an executive to keep out of hot water in the future.

While painful tasks have to be performed and occasions arise which call for adverse executive decisions on some of the proposals and requests made by members of the staff, it should be emphasized that the work of an executive is not primarily negative. On the contrary the opportunities for positive action heavily predominate.

Maintaining perspective

It takes a broad perspective, a level head, and a steadfast eye for an executive to choose effectively from the questions before him those with which he will deal immediately, those on which he will defer judgment, and those which properly can be delegated to his lieutenants for decision. As already has been remarked, the daily administrative tasks, which commonly consume three quarters or more of the time and energy of a chief executive officer, are not dramatic, but because of their very number they tax an executive's ability to maintain perspective. The lesser problems which come in a never ceasing flow cannot safely be ignored or neglected because they immediately affect the effectiveness with which current operations are maintained. The larger, more general problems, which seemingly are not so pressing, also cannot safely be neglected, for they are likely to have a vital bearing on the successful continuance of operations in the future.

Not long ago a case came to my attention of a company in which the chief executive deprecated "the drive" which he observed in many other companies. He received practically no operating reports and did not follow daily operations closely. Aside from consideration of questions of policy which the department heads occasionally brought to him at their discretion, he devoted his attention to labor relations. He allowed each department head to go his own way. "If each man is allowed to find his own level," he said, "to express himself as he sees fit, I think that in the long run we can accomplish more and have a better time doing it than if we were working under pressure."

This executive had held his position for about three years. The company was family owned, and he had become president upon the death of his uncle. The company was prosperous, but certain disquieting signs were beginning to appear. Lateness in making deliveries to customers, for example, was becoming more frequent, and as a consequence the patronage of two large customers already had been lost. Control was loose, and some of the men in the organization were uncertain and confused as to just what their responsibilities were. These unwholesome developments were ominous for the welfare of the company and all its employees as well as for the owners.

This executive had a concept of administration directly in contrast to that of an executive who becomes so immersed in daily details that he has no time for attending to major problems. In order to attain maximum results, both types of questions require executive attention, and one of the tests of executive capacity is the ability to maintain a proper perspective in dealing with the whole range of problems pressing for decision.

The ability to maintain proper perspective is continually being tested in other ways in most administrative positions. An executive frequently is called upon, for example, to judge whether a particular situation calls for immediate decision or for watchful waiting. When a competitor announces an advance in prices, for instance, shall a company follow immediately or will it be better strategy to defer such action, at least temporarily?

Despite the constant urge to get things done, there are times when it is better for an executive to "keep his shirt on," when the possible gain from immediate action is more than offset by the advantages which will accrue from proceeding more deliberately. There are executives who make a fetish of deciding every question quickly and who therefore frequently go off half-cocked. There are other executives who are so cautious that essential action often is unduly deferred. The capacity to determine wisely in each situation at it arises whether to act quickly and incisively or to proceed deliberately involves judgment of a rather uncommon type.

As has been suggested in preceding chapters, the capacity for selecting, instructing, and coaching lieutenants and the capacity for keeping himself informed are significant qualifications for executive achievement. The ability to perform the daily tasks required for keeping the wheels turning and the maintenance of a proper perspective in the daily drive also are significant executive qualifications. Still other executive attributes will be discussed in the chapters to follow.

VI

Survival in a Changing World

In the preceding chapter attention was focused on the daily tasks involved in directing operations. We turn now to another type of problem, that of meeting changing conditions. We live and our businesses are operated in an ever changing world. Change has been pervasive for many centuries in the past, and I can see no grounds for expecting changes to be less frequent or less severe in the future. Business executives will continue to operate in a dynamic, changing environment.

Technological change

The technological innovations which have occurred during the last two hundred years have been so numerous and so frequent that there is a wealth of examples from which to choose. Those which are cited here are not necessarily the most significant, but they serve for purposes of illustration.

Radio communication received a great impetus during the First World War, and in the 1920's the commercial development of the industry went on apace. Improvements in transmission and reception techniques reached a point which made feasible the introduction of network broadcasting early in 1927. A new industry had sprung up, providing employment to thousands of persons in the manufacture of equipment and receiving sets, in the retailing and servicing of the sets, and in the manifold activities of broadcasting.

The growth of the radio industry had widely ramifying effects. Temporarily at least it served to curtail the sales of pianos and largely destroyed the market for player pianos. It was simpler and less expensive to switch on the radio than to buy and operate a player piano. Radio sets also competed with many other items for a share of the consumer's dollar.

The growth of radio broadcasting was made possible by technological achievements, but its commercial success resulted from its utilization for advertising purposes. The amounts spent for radio advertising, however, were offset by a reduction of expenditures for advertising in magazines and newspapers.[1] Thus the growth of the radio industry had a heavy impact on the magazine and newspaper publishing industries.

Now comes television. Another new industry, closely related to radio, is developing. It likewise is affording an opportunity for new enterprises to develop and for some established companies to grow. It likewise seems destined to have far-reaching effects on other industries. The executives of companies which, as advertisers, have been sponsoring big radio programs have to decide whether to shift to television and at what time. By plunging early they may gain preferred positions on the broadcasting schedules, but at this stage the cost is heavy and the advantage to be gained may not be worth the sacrifice.

The producers and exhibitors of moving pictures also are disturbed by television. Will television seriously cut into the attendance at moving picture theaters? The manufacturers of home furnishings, in contrast, are hopeful that television,

[1] Neil H. Borden, Malcolm D. Taylor, and Howard T. Hovde, *National Advertising in Newspapers* (Cambridge: Harvard University Press, 1946), p. 35.

by inducing people to spend more time at home in the evening, may revive an interest in attractive home furnishings, a market which has suffered from interindustry competition for the last thirty years.

Transportation is another field in which there are many examples of the impacts of technological change. In the nineteenth century the railroad supplanted the stagecoach, the covered wagon, and the canal boat in providing for transportation of persons and merchandise. The railroad made possible the opening up of vast new regions for settlement, and it widened marketing areas so as to render large-scale manufacturing operations practical for many industries.

Then came the passenger automobile, the bus, and the truck, which have cut heavily into the business of the railroads. The manufacturing, marketing, and servicing of automobiles, busses, and trucks have become major industries, and directly or indirectly they have affected almost every other industry in this country. They have provided a vast market for steel, tin, rubber, glass, upholstery, and many other materials. They have given rise to new industries, such as those manufacturing accessories and antifreeze compounds, and they have dotted the highways with filling stations and hot-dog stands. They have necessitated the building and maintenance of thousands of miles of hard-surfaced roads.

The growth of the automotive industries brought new opportunities to many enterprises but ruined others. The manufacturers of buggies and harnesses, for instance, had to shift to the making of other products or go out of business. Many did go out of business. The breeders of horses lost much of their market. And the village blacksmith shop vanished — the village blacksmith shop with carts and buggies parked outside and with horses lined up inside, in a murky atmosphere of acrid smoke and a pungent odor of seared hoofs, waiting to be shod by the sooty, sweaty smith clad in his leather apron. In the retail hardware store, nearby one of these village blacksmith shops, where I had my first business job, the kegs of horseshoes and bars of iron with which I wrestled as a boy no longer are items in the inventory. A gasoline filling station now stands on the site of the old blacksmith shop.

The automobile and the bus cut into the traffic of the steam railroads, and they also drove many local street railways into bankruptcy. The increased use of automobiles also caused major shifts in retail trade in the United States. Before the First World War most families made the bulk of their purchases within ten miles of their homes. Before the end of the 1920's the trading radius of many families had widened to fifty or a hundred miles, and the retail trade for certain types of goods tended to center at the county seats or larger cities, to the detriment of small-town merchants and the wholesalers who supplied them. By rendering shopping centers more accessible to rural and small-town consumers, the automobile was a factor in causing the big mail-order houses to open chains of retail stores. And in the grocery trade, the family automobile contributed to the growth of chain stores by facilitating cash-and-carry operations. The traffic congestion in our large cities, caused by automotive vehicles, furthermore, has given rise to problems for local governments and urban business firms for which they are still struggling to find a satisfactory solution. Thus the effects of the new method of transportation have ramified.

During the last twenty years the airplane also has added to the woes of the railroads by cutting into their passenger traffic. The automobile hit the short-run traffic, whereas the bus and the airplane hit the long-distance travel. Under the spurs of competition from automotive vehicles and airplanes, the railroads, perhaps belatedly, have responded with streamlined trains and other modernizations. And these struggles are by no means yet concluded.

The petroleum industry likewise affords examples of the unsettling impacts of technological changes. In order to provide fuel for gasoline engines in automobiles, busses, trucks, and other equipment, a vast refining industry was developed. Kerosene, once the main product of the petroleum industry, became a relatively insignificant item for the refiners. A by-product of gasoline refining was heavy oil which seemed to have a market only as fuel. The installation of oil burning equipment was stimulated in order to provide a sales outlet for fuel oil. Now the demand for fuel oil is so great that it no longer is a by-product. It constitutes one of the main products of the refining industry.

The growth of demand for fuel oil, as in the case of changes in other industries cited, has made possible the building up of new manufacturing and marketing businesses, and it also has had ramified effects. In the industrial field oil has extensively supplanted bituminous coal for heating the boilers in manufacturing plants and commercial buildings. On the railroads within the last ten years and particularly since 1945, oil-burning Diesels have replaced a substantial number of coal-burning locomotives. The demand for Diesels, in fact, has given a new lease on life to the locomotive manufacturing companies.

The competition between industries stimulated by technological change is relentless.

The shift to fuel oil for heating private homes, particularly in the northeastern section of the United States, has furnished a large market for new oil-burning equipment. And thereby it has struck a heavy blow at the anthracite coal-mining industry. For a long period of years until about 1925, the anthracite coal companies appeared to be in an impregnable position. By 1936 they were struggling for existence. The increased use of gas and electricity for cooking also had contributed to the decline in the demand for anthracite coal. And manufacturers of coal stoves and ranges, once a prosperous industry, either had shifted to the manufacture of other products or were facing a threat of extinction.

Ice-making machinery, to cite still another example, destroyed the harvesting of natural ice on Maine rivers for shipment to New York and other large cities in four-masted sailing vessels. That machinery likewise destroyed a once-lucrative trade in exporting ice from Massachusetts to India. Then came the mechanical refrigerator to cut into the ice-machinery business and to worsen the lot of the ice man.

A century ago the mowing machine was inaugurating a revolutionary mechanization of agriculture, followed by the reaper, the "combine," and many other farm machines. Now a mechanical cotton picker is coming into use, in order to permit the survival of a cotton-growing industry in the "old South." The mechanical cotton picker, together with other technological changes in cotton growing, bids fair to revolutionize the economic, social, and business life of a large agricultural area.

The troubles of the cotton growers stem in part from the expansion of the rayon industry. Rayon was first known as artificial silk, but during the last thirty years it has taken a place as a major textile material. Rayon and nylon together have struck the natural-silk industry a mortal blow. The weavers have been able to shift over to the new fibers, but the raw-silk growers of China and Japan have lost their major markets. And as the cost of making rayon has been reduced and the quality improved, that fiber has been usurping a larger and larger share of the market for raw cotton. Cotton no longer is "king," and cotton growers, like numerous other farmers, have sought government aid as a buffer against changing conditions.

One could go on almost endlessly citing technological changes which are of significance to business management — such as the development of synthetic rubber, plastics, insulating materials, the spray gun for painting, unit-drive electric motors (competing with leather belts), material-handling equipment, office machinery, the flotation process for treating nonferrous ores, and many, many others. Enough examples have been cited, however, to demonstrate that even though the new developments may be different for different industries both as to their nature and their velocity, nevertheless technological change is one of the facts of business life which constantly must be reckoned with in every industry. And technological change is only one of the frequently shifting elements in the environment in which the business executive operates.

Shifts in demand

Some shifts in consumer demand and in consumer buying habits, as has been indicated in the preceding section, have been generated by technological innovations. Other shifts in demand are independent of technological changes or are brought about only in part by such changes. A few examples will serve to illustrate this type of change.

Between 1901 and 1919 Cluett, Peabody & Company built up a substantial business in the production and sale of starched collars. That company was far and away the leader in its field, and its sales, the bulk of which were collars, amounted to $32,422,000 in 1919. During the following five years, however, men decided in increasing numbers to wear collar-attached shirts, and the collar business began to skid. Cluett, Peabody & Company, faced with this shift in demand, decided to go into the shirt business on a large scale. The company previously had made over two thirds of the collars manufactured in the United States and had only a few competitors. In the shirt business the company faced about nine hundred competing manufacturers, many of them small operators. Because of that shift in demand the company had to build a new organization and to modify drastically its production and marketing operations.

The manufacturers of men's hats recently seem to have become apprehensive of a decline in the demand for their products. Whenever a hat manufacturer sees a group of young men bareheaded on the street, he shivers.

Men continue to wear underwear, but over a period of years there has been a considerable shift in demand from knit fabrics to shorts made from woven cloth. What the knitters have lost the weavers have gained. Closed automobiles and central heating systems in homes have been among the factors which caused this shift in demand.

Many items of women's wearing apparel, of course, are fashion merchandise, subject to continual and frequent changes in style. Style changes are an inherent characteristic of the fashion industries, however, and do not belong in the same category with the shifts in demand to which attention is being directed here. But some items of women's wear do exemplify major long-run shifts in demand. Several years ago the demand for women's knit underwear, for example, also declined, being replaced with items not necessary to describe.

Cotton hosiery is another article once commonly worn by women. Thirty years ago there was a large market for women's cotton hosiery, knit on circular machines. In the 1920's, partly as a result of the vogue of short skirts and partly in consequence of economic prosperity, the demand shifted to silk hosiery knit on full-fashioned machines, and several companies equipped to make the unwanted seamless cotton hosiery were forced into liquidation.

In the 1920's likewise the demand for cotton-warp worsteds shifted to all-wool fabrics, and at least two large mills which for years had concentrated on the production of cotton-warp goods had to scramble into the production of other fabrics. The cotton-warp fabrics had been largely standardized staples. The new fabrics which these mills undertook to manufacture were style goods, and the managers of those mills presently found themselves facing a strange new set of problems.

About the same time the demand for gingham cloth, a fabric woven from dyed and bleached yarns on box looms, shifted to printed fabrics. The Amoskeag mills in Manchester, New Hampshire, one of the largest cotton mills in the United States, the Boston Manufacturing Company in Waltham, Massachusetts, where the first power loom in the United States was installed, and the Lancaster mills, with a very modern plant in Clinton, Massachusetts, were among the victims of this adverse shift in demand. They were equipped to make ginghams, and when the demand for those goods dropped, they could not economically utilize their box looms for weaving other goods.

In food industries long-term changes in demand have been taking place over a period of years. With changes in occupations and in living habits, there has been a decline in the per capita demand for wheat and potatoes, for example, and an increase in the per capita demand for dairy products and for fruits and fruit juices. Then there have been the increased sales of packaged foods, branded and widely advertised. In some instances these packaged foods were new items; in other instances package sales took the place of bulk sales. The old cracker barrel, for example, has long since disappeared from the retail grocery store. Food processors, wholesalers, and retailers all have felt the impact of these shifts in demand.

A few other examples out of many which could be listed are the following. Frozen foods have been altering the trade in fresh fruit, vegetables, and meat, with effects on growers, processors, and distributors. Beer cans compete with beer bottles. Candy bars have cut heavily into the sales of bulk confectionery. A shift in demand in the late 1920's enabled Chevrolet and Chrysler to become close competitors of Ford when Mr. Ford persisted in clinging overlong to his old Model T. Now large-scale attempts are being made to develop a demand for prefabricated houses, which, if successful, would have far-reaching effects on the whole sprawling construction industry.

The causes for these shifts in demand are manifold — technological influences, occupational changes, new living conditions, changes in the levels of income and prices, advertising and sales promotion of manufacturers and merchants, and sometimes new surges of fancy which seem to be almost spontaneous in their origin. Whatever the causes may be, these shifts in demand vitally affect the job of a business executive.

Managerial innovations

Under managerial innovations may be included such developments as time studies for setting work standards, line production methods, the rise of the "lifo" (last-in-first-out) method of inventory accounting, packaging of products, self-service arrangements in chain stores and supermarkets, department store branches, vending machines, merger movements, establishment of research departments, retirement programs for executives and personnel, and of course many others. All such changes add to the instability of the environment in which the executive must carry on his work.

These managerial innovations put executive ability to a particularly searching test — the test of being able to discriminate between substance and form. The common human desires to conform to the style, to keep up with the neighbors, to be credited with being progressive, sometimes impel the acceptance of an innovation for a business to which it is not suited.

Soon after time and motion studies had been introduced successfully in certain factories for setting work standards, various other companies attempted to use the same devices but without the preparatory steps which had been taken in the successful plants. The crude attempts at time and motion studies in the aping establishments caused so much resentment among the workers that hostility to the use of the devices became rather widespread. The aping establishments got the form but not the substance and spirit of the innovations.

After line production methods had achieved such conspicuous success in the production of automobiles, various companies in other industries where conditions were markedly different undiscriminatingly undertook to apply line production methods to their operations. A candy manufacturing company, for example, turning out a wide variety of products, oftentimes in relatively small batches, built a new plant laid out to operate on a line production basis. The result was to introduce rigidity into a situation where flexibility was essential. In another case, a company manufacturing machines for which there was a widely fluctuating demand built an expensive new plant laid out for line production. It likewise undiscriminatingly copied the methods of another industry not suited to its own.

A grocery chain-store company has been following the trend of the last few years by concentrating more and more of its operations in supermarkets, but its profits have lessened. The company apparently has failed to adjust its managerial organization and policies to the supermarket type of operation. It has the form but not the understanding of the new type of enterprise.

In 1919–20, when labor conditions were widely unsettled, there was a fad for establishing personnel departments in industry. In numerous instances the functions to be performed were not fully thought through, and the personnel managers were selected on a rather hit-or-miss basis. Such personnel departments were short-lived, and the bad taste from those ill-conceived ventures lingered for many years after their demise. In other instances, however, where the purpose and methods of sound personnel management were really understood, the departments had a continuing and helpful experience.

During the last five years there has been a popular move to establish technical research departments in industry, partly at least as a result of the conspicuous success attained by DuPont, Union Carbide, General Electric, Corning Glass Works, and several other companies through their research departments. I have no adequate basis for expressing an opinion, but I suspect that some of these new research departments are window dressing, which will disappear as competition stiffens.

It is a temptation to keep on citing examples, but the ones which have been given probably will suffice to illustrate the prevalence of managerial innovations and to exemplify the possible confusion between substance and form in the introduction of such innovations.

In concluding this section I wish to point out that there are executives who discriminate shrewdly in determining which of the managerial innovations they will try out in their companies and in adapting the new managerial devices to the needs of their situations. I have had a long acquaintance with some of these discriminating executives, and I consider their ability to distinguish between form and substance to be one of their outstanding qualifications for leadership.

Finally, it may not be amiss for me to add that the confusion between form and substance is not uncommon in academic quarters. In fact it sometimes seems that it has been one of my missions in life to remind some of my colleagues from time to time that the variety of offerings in a curriculum is of far less consequence than the quality of the instruction. Whether this or that particular topic is added usually is of minor importance. The real problem is to make sure that whatever is offered is well taught. Like business concerns, furthermore, some educational institutions indulge in window dressing. They are impelled to copy, in a somewhat mechanistic and slavish manner, the programs of other institutions, providing the form but sometimes missing the substance.

Economic, social, and political changes

Business management is highly sensitive to the economic, social, and political climate in which it operates. And that climate is continually undergoing modification.

Business depressions, such as those which began in 1873, 1893, 1907, 1920, and 1929, are nightmares to those who lived through them. In between those major depressions minor recessions also have occurred. Unemployment, idle plants, financial losses, and floods of bankruptcies accompanied the major depressions, and similar though less severe results came with the recessions.

In the light of past experience, it seems certain that major fluctuations in business activity will recur in the future. Progress has been made, to be sure, in the analysis and study of business cycles, but our knowledge of the causes of depressions is far from complete.

In the United States attempts are being made through legislative and administrative measures to prevent economic slumps and abnormal unemployment. Unfortunately these measures cannot be divorced from current political expediency. When the federal budget cannot be balanced in a period of high business activity, for example, it is naïve to assume that the business cycle can be controlled by governmental action. Certain theories promulgated during the last twenty years for alleviating business depressions by government spending have provided a pretext, if any were needed, for maintaining government expenditures continuously at a high level. The effect of such spending policies is inflationary, and inflation is one of the surest breeders of depressions.

For the last ten years many business executives have been almost constantly apprehensive of a severe setback in business activity. That attitude of apprehension has been a healthy one. It has helped to discourage indulgence in speculative practices which otherwise might have occurred.

In facing the uncertainties of fluctuations in business activity, the chief points on which business executives can be most certain are the following. First, there is no simple, mechanistic formula for forecasting a business depression. Everlasting watchfulness, careful analysis, and dispassionate judgment may provide a warning, but there are no easy means of being certain.

Second, whenever a spirit of optimism becomes so pervasive in business and government circles that the danger of a depression is lightly brushed aside or ignored, then is the time to be particularly cautious. Whenever the whole crowd heads in one direction, the shrewd man is likely to be going the other way.

Third, the major problem for the business executive is to be properly prepared to weather an economic reversal, whenever it comes. Preparedness is the surest means for survival.

If a large number of business concerns are soundly prepared for a shock, the severity of the shock, when it does come, will be substantially lightened.

Fourth, unless government policies, which have become a much larger factor during the last twenty years, are directed toward preventing depressions rather than merely alleviating them, those policies in the end are likely to make matters worse.

Fifth, the forces which generate a major business reversal are manifold and some of them are world-wide in their origin. Many of those forces work slowly as well as relentlessly, and the seeds of a depression are sown five to ten years before the reaction occurs.

Price levels constitute another variable element in the economic environment in which a business executive must make his decisions. From 1897 to 1920, for example, the general trend of commodity prices was upward, as a result of the opening up of new gold mines, the application of a new process for extracting gold from ore, and governmental credit policies. After 1920 followed a period of downward trend, culminating in the depressed thirties. Since 1933 prices have swung upward again, the rise being greatly accelerated, of course, by the inflation of the Second World War.

The building of a new plant is an example of decisions particularly affected by changes in the price level. Because a plant normally has a life of upwards of ten years, the initial cost of the plant and the resultant charges for depreciation affect the relative strength of a company in meeting the competition of other companies which have built their plants at higher or lower price levels. At the present time the depreciation reserves accumulated from the write-offs on plants built twenty or twenty-five years ago are far from adequate for financing the building of new plants to replace the old ones.

When changes in the price level take place, manufacturers whose products are sold at customary retail prices, such as chewing gum, soft drinks, and various other items, experience changing costs but unchanging selling prices. In department stores it is a customary practice to sell certain types of cotton garments at $4.95, $5.95, $7.95, and so on — "Price-lining," it is called. As the general level of prices changes, the stores seek to adhere to their price lines and to maintain their standard markups. Consequently the quality of the fabric is modified. I never have received a satisfactory explanation as to why it is more advantageous to vary quality than to alter prices, but that is only one of many mysteries in department store operation which I have never had an opportunity to fathom.

As an example of the sort of unpredictable change which occurs in government policy, the Federal Trade Commission's theory of "conscious parallel action" may be cited. For over twenty years certain members of the staff of the Federal Trade Commission and their economic advisers had been developing new theories to support their crusade against the basing-point method of quoting prices and against the use of delivered prices which in effect involved assumption by the seller of part of the cost of delivering merchandise in competitive markets. In Count II of the Rigid Steel Conduit case the respondents were charged with using an unfair method of competition by selling at prices which yielded varying mill net returns; in other words, in selling at delivered prices and assuming part of the cost of delivering the merchandise to customers in territories where competitors had a differential freight advantage.

In its briefs and in its arguments before the lower courts, counsel for the Federal Trade Commission repeatedly stated that there was no charge of conspiracy between the respondents in Count II of the complaint. Counsel for the Commission, however, did charge not only the other respondents but also two rigid steel conduit manufacturers against whom charges of conspiracy under Count I had been dismissed with violation of the law through "conscious parallel action." And in the pleadings before the Supreme Court, counsel for the Commission explained, in substance, that "conscious parallel action" is something short of conspiracy which amounts to conspiracy. In other words, the respondents were not guilty of conspiracy under this Count but were accused of being guilty of what amounted to the same thing.

The Supreme Court divided four to four in that case, with one justice not participating, with the result that the Commission's weird doctrine of "conscious parallel action" became established, at least temporarily, as law. Under that doctrine, a company which quite independently introduces a new and effective means of competition that in itself is legal may become a violator of the law merely through the action of competitors who consciously adopt the same method of competition.

The application of the theory of "conscious parallel action" is but one example of the changes being wrought by administrative agencies of the federal government and their legal staffs. A prevalent tendency of the Supreme Court, furthermore, to disregard precedents in reviewing cases which come before it facilitates the procedures of the administrative agencies. Long-established legal guideposts thereby have become less dependable for the conduct of business management.

As at so many other points in this chapter, it would be possible to go on and on citing examples. But my purpose is to show how prevalent and how varied are the changes in the business environment in which an executive and his lieutenants perform their tasks, rather than to catalogue all the illustrations which could be given.

Shifts from agricultural to industrial employment, with consequent greater urbanization of population, geographical shifts in population, changes in the standard of living, which particularly influence shifts in demand, the rise of labor unions, the conflicts between unions, labor legislation, social security laws, taxation on corporations and on personal incomes, excise taxes, sales taxes, and local taxes, and other governmental administrative and regulatory policies — all these are also major features of the economic, social, and political climate in which business operates, and they are all subject to change with greater or less frequency, sometimes with little advance warning.

From the foregoing review it appears that the most certain aspect of an uncertain world is that changes will continually be encountered. The problem for the business executive is how to survive in such an ever changing environment.

Whistling in the dark

Changes are unpleasant. In their mildest forms, changes in environment upset routines and necessitate inconvenient readjustments. In their virulent manifestations, changes are revolutionary or even devastating.

When a baffling change puts in an appearance, there seems to be a natural tendency among some business executives to start whistling in the dark. The following examples are manifestations of that tendency.

In 1917, when passenger automobiles were coming to be more widely used and the jitneys, which had begun operations in 1914, were being supplanted by busses, the following statement was made: "Finally, the same consolation obtains with the interurban railway as with the city railway. Undoubtedly the interurban manager will find that travel begets travel and that the conveniences of the automobile will cause many people to reside in the country, a fact which should ultimately be of benefit to the interurban electric railway in both its passenger and freight business." [2]

In 1931, when the raw-silk industry was experiencing vicissitudes, the following statement about competition from rayon, then still sometimes referred to as artificial silk, appeared: "It seems that, right up to the most recent years, the introduction of artificial silk has reacted favorably rather than adversely on the consumption of natural silk, seeing that, owing to the cheapness of artificial silk, it has produced a taste for silk stuffs and manufactured goods amongst all classes of the population." [3]

In a prospectus issued by the American Piano Company in May 1927, in connection with an offering of the company's stock for sale, the president of the company stated: "The increasing use of pianos, especially those of high quality, and reproducing pianos, is partly the result of the country's growing wealth and high standards of living, but has also been stimulated by the more general appreciation of good music fostered by the radio, the phonograph, and the moving picture theatre." In December 1929, the company went into receivership. The failure of the company was caused only in part, of course, by the competition of radio, but that competition was a substantial factor, the sales of reproducing pianos being particularly hard hit.

In 1932 a representative of a company which manufactured ice-making machinery informed me that the ice business would enjoy greater prosperity because of the demand for all sorts of household refrigeration being stimulated by the advertising and sales promotional work of the manufacturers of mechanical refrigerators. The ice men were whistling in the dark.

[2] Henry W. Blake and Walter Jackson, *Electric Railway Transportation* (New York: McGraw-Hill, 1917), pp. 353–354.

[3] E. G. Guimont, "Natural Silk," *Index* (Stockholm: Svenska Handelsbanken, August 1931), p. 184.

In an article in *Collier's* in 1943 it was stated with reference to air transport:

> As to fares, there will be two, possibly three, classes. For long distance, luxury, nonstop service, you will pay extra. Even that, air-traffic men say, will be only equivalent to rail fare plus Pullman. Third-class fares might undercut present rail fares. This does not mean that air travel will supplant or even harm rail or bus travel. It's been transportation history that the more travel facilities there are, the more travel there is.
>
> Competition will force all means of travel, surface and air, to readjust fares healthily; and there will be more business for all.[4]

The optimism expressed in the foregoing quotation has not been supported by the experience of the transportation companies. So far as the railroads are concerned, furthermore, the old bugaboo of competition from trucks has been particularly troublesome of late, and during the last couple of years I have heard several railroad executives whistling in the dark.

In 1949 a representative of the moving-picture industry informed me that the producers and exhibitors of moving pictures were hopeful that television, instead of cutting down attendance at the theaters, would stimulate an interest which would lead to larger attendances. They apparently were puckering up to whistle the familiar tune.

I deem it a remarkable coincidence that so many persons in so many industries over such a period of years have whistled the same tune. I suspect, furthermore, that historical research would reveal many more instances, over a much longer period of time, in which the same tune has been heard.

There are other tunes also, of course, which are whistled in the dark. Certain business executives and lawyers, for instance, have a very bitter tune in which they execrate various governmental policies and their sponsors. This might be

[4] *Collier's* (June 1943), p. 74.

called the apoplectic tune. I have a great deal of sympathy with some of their views, but I do not enjoy the tune which they whistle.

Whistling in the dark provides no assurance of survival in a changing world.

Survival through adaptation

In this chapter it has been demonstrated at considerable length that the environment in which a business enterprise operates is continually subject to change. Since these changes, in many instances, are inexorable, survival is possible only for those enterprises which can adapt themselves to new conditions.

The companies which have been outstandingly successful in continuously adapting their operations to changed conditions commonly have effected the adaptations in an undramatic manner. In substance, the executives of those companies have taken these environmental changes in stride. They have accepted readjustments to new conditions as inevitable, albeit sometimes annoying, concomitants of their administrative work. Success of a business corporation over a considerable period of time usually is evidence of adaptive ability in its management. Many such corporations now have large resources. Even though the executives of some of those companies are so accustomed to the process of adaptation that they often ascribe the prosperity of their companies to more tangible but perhaps less vital factors, nevertheless the adaptive ability of their managements has been a major factor in the building up of their resources.

The first step in adaptation is to be informed on the facts and the next step is to face the facts squarely and promptly, without wishful thinking and without yielding to the temptation of tinkering. Some examples of wishful thinking have been cited where there was whistling in the dark. As regards tinkering, that is a particularly common approach to the problems of readjustment when the nature of the problems is not comprehended or when there is a lack of courage to face the facts.

A couple of examples will illustrate tinkering. A company operating a large restaurant in the business district of a midwestern city experienced a decline in patronage because of adverse business conditions and because of a shift in the location of a substantial part of the business district. The executives assumed that their major problem was one of increasing sales. Consequently they opened a string of restaurants. But the resultant increase in sales did not restore profits. The executives for some time were reluctant to face the fact that the original restaurant building was a white elephant. There was not sufficient patronage to support it in its old location, and it was poorly situated to serve as a commissary for a real chain of restaurants. A competing chain, for example, could gain a substantial advantage by locating its commissary in a low-rent district, relatively free from traffic congestion. Tinkering with new sales schemes did not solve the company's basic problem of adaptation.

In another case, the executives of a company manufacturing factory tools in three scattered plants stated that their major problem was sales, whereas an analysis of such meager information as the company possessed indicated that its difficulties lay in the lack of a central order department and a lack of specialization in the plants where short runs of improperly allocated orders were constantly being put through. The executives of that company were tinkering with sales experiments when the problem lay in headquarters organization.

In contrast to these makeshift attempts to meet unforeseen situations, the policy of a company such as General Electric is especially notable. Immediately after its organization, General Electric Company began to set aside large reserves to take care of the obsolescence of plant and equipment. These reserves for obsolescence were in addition to the amounts reserved for normal depreciation. Some thirty years later, in its annual report for 1926, for instance, the company stated that it had "followed the policy of providing a general plant reserve in excess of normal depreciation rates, so as to enable it to take promptly out of service buildings or equipment, which, although not worn out physically, are inefficient and uneconomical. Failure to provide such a reserve would make the management much slower to abandon inefficient buildings and machinery, and would make the company less able to meet new conditions, and, therefore, less effective in economical production and in competition."

That is but one example of the astute foresightedness which has been shown by the executives of that company over a period of nearly sixty years, a foresightedness which has been one of the major factors in the growth and prosperity of the company. General Electric now is a large company, but large companies have no monoply on the exercise of foresight. Large or small, the companies which survive and prosper for any extended period of time usually are those whose executives foresightedly adapt their policies and their practices continually to the meeting of new situations.

Not every new situation, to be sure, is likely to be met successfully by every company. So long as new technological developments are permitted to occur, so long as consumers are allowed freedom to buy what they will, with resultant shifts in demand, so long as the government is permitted to follow inflationary or deflationary policies and to make substantial changes in the rules under which business operates, so long as these and other changes occur, some business failures will take place, with the sad aftermath of lost jobs and lost investments. With real leadership, however, the frequency of failures can be lessened. And in those situations where no means of adaptation can be found to permit survival, orderly liquidation, with a minimum wastage of assets, is more likely to be possible if the facts are faced frankly and promptly.

As I see it, there are two ways of looking at this changing world. One is that of morbid martyrdom, with a feeling of being faced by overwhelming problems and of being ground down inevitably by the inescapable forces of change. The other way of viewing the changing conditions is to see in them a challenge, an environment to be conquered. For those who have the imagination, the foresight, and the courage to accept it, the challenge of the environment is full of zest. So long as environmental conditions are subject to change, so long will there be frontiers for pioneer leadership.

The imagination which leads to an understanding of the changing environment, the flexibility of mind which permits the acceptance of new points of view, and the courage to face the facts, all are qualities of an executive leader.

When some of my friends are feeling particularly pessimistic and martyred, I occasionally read the following quotation to them:

More than a hundred years ago, a distinguished French physician, writing to an intimate friend the day after his son, Alex, was born, said: ". . . The poor infant enters the world in very troubled times . . . Conditions of life are daily becoming more difficult. Nannette, our servant, has paid 23 sous for half a kilo of butter and 2 sous for each fresh egg. It is absurd and exorbitant. I would like to see my son embracing the noble career of medicine but I see quite well that he cannot. One of the heads of the faculty has confided to me that this profession is literally invaded, and then this madness of speed is wearing out men. Only yesterday I saw a post chaise tearing along. It makes one giddy. The horses were galloping at more than five leagues an hour and everyone wants his carriage. The streets of Paris are so congested that you must wait a long time if you wish to cross them. Madness of the century, my dear friend, for which men will pay in the brevity of their days! My son, like his contemporaries, will not live to be old. We know not what his future has in store for him, but we can bet with certainty on his not becoming a centenarian." After 1832 things improved in spite of Dr. Guemot's prediction and his son, Dr. Alexander Guemot, about whom this letter was written, was honored by the French Academy of Medicine on his one hundredth birthday.[5]

[5] *Business Conditions Weekly* (October 20, 1934).

VII

The Spirit of Risk-Taking

In this chapter I propose to review briefly the hazards by which business management is encompassed, to note the relation of those hazards to losses and profits, to evaluate some of the efforts to attain security in a hazardous world, and to draw a few general conclusions anent risk-taking.

Managerial hazards and risks

Technological developments, shifts in demand, the introduction of managerial innovations, the discovery of new ways of doing business, the ups and downs of business activity, and numerous other economic, social, and political changes, as set forth at length in the preceding chapter, constitute perils and hazards for business management. The dangers emanating from such changes in the operating environment are ever present. At any one time for an individual enterprise some of these hazards are more dangerous than others. Nevertheless, it would be difficult, I believe, to find a single business concern over fifteen years old which has not at some time encountered every hazard in the gamut.

In addition to these environmental hazards, other managerial risks have been indicated or implied in the discussions of other topics. For example, in the selection of a lieutenant a risk oftentimes is involved. There is likely to be some uncertainty as to whether a new appointee can fully measure up to the requirements of the job, as to whether he can establish effective working relationships with his colleagues and with his subordinates, and as to whether he will be fully amenable to instruction and developmental guidance. Despite the utmost care in choosing lieutenants, it has been my observation that inevitably mistakes occasionally are made.

When a mistake has been made in the selection of a key man for the organization and the mistake ultimately is recognized, the problem of deciding how to correct it may be a tough one, particularly when the misfit has an impressive personality. If he was promoted from within, it seldom is a satisfactory means of correcting the mistake to return the misfit to his former position. In the first place, the morale of a man demoted is likely to be impaired. He will have suffered a loss of self-confidence, and his ambitions will have been thwarted. Of no less consequence, he will have incurred a loss of esteem among his associates and subordinates, a loss which will weaken his effectiveness in dealing with them. A man who has failed inevitably finds it difficult to reëstablish his authority within the same organization.

In the second place, long before a mistake in promotion has become so apparent that corrective action is warranted, the misfit's former position ordinarily will have been filled, and a whole chain of promotions and shifts in personnel will have taken place. The misfit cannot be returned to his old job without upsetting these new arrangements, thereby causing disappointments, resentments and even feelings that there has been a lack of good faith. It is almost axiomatic in business administration that a mistake in promotion, particularly in the higher administrative echelons, cannot be corrected by demotion. That axiom is well founded.

When a mistake is made in the selection of a man from outside to fill a key position, that mistake also seldom can be corrected by moving the misfit to some lower position. He not only has to live down the possible resentment against his first appointment, but if his demotion were to start knocking people off the rungs all the way down the organizational ladder, his task of securing acceptance of himself as a supervisor would be almost insuperable. A man brought in from outside to fill a key position either must make good or get out.

Thus the selection of men to fill key positions involves the risk of mistakes, the correction of which may be painful. Any such mistake also is costly from a profit-and-loss standpoint.

An alternative to the demotion or firing of an administrative misfit is a drifting course. That procedure, which is not an uncommon one, involves a moral risk — the risk of sacrificing the broader interests of the enterprise to the personal comfort of the executive who is reluctant to perform a painful task. A drifting procedure also is costly since effectiveness of operations is thereby impaired. The administrative organization cannot achieve maximum results when any of its parts do not fit.

There is one other hazard involved in the employment of key personnel, a hazard which does not occur with high frequency but which nevertheless is far from rare. That is the hazard of mental illness, an affliction which develops gradually, with insidious effects, and one with which it is especially difficult to deal. A few years ago the president of a midwestern manufacturing company, for example, began to notice that his sales manager was manifesting strange attitudes. Both men had worked together in close harmony and intimate friendship for many years, and the sales manager was the number-two man in the organization. One manifestation of his affliction was an increasing hostility toward the president, a bitter unwillingness to coöperate in the normal manner. At times he seemed to contemplate personal violence. The president had not in any way changed his procedures or his attitude. The sales manager had become mentally ill. Until the ill man could be persuaded to enter a sanatorium, the president of the company lived through an anguishing experience. Such illnesses occur frequently enough to warrant reference to them as one of the occupational risks with which any executive may have to deal. One who has not lived through such ordeals cannot have much comprehension of the agony which they cause. The executive is torn between loyalty, friendship, and sympathy for the individual on the one hand, and, on the other, his duties for safeguarding the interests of the enterprise entrusted to his management.

Let us turn now to a brief consideration of other types of risk, such as those, for example, which arise in the day-to-day operations of a business. As was pointed out early in this volume, administration is a decision-making process. That statement indicates the pervasiveness of risk, because in almost every problem on which a decision must be made there is at least a latent opportunity to err. The following problems illustrate this sort of risk.

When a new plant is built, a mistake can be make in determining its size and location. If it is too large, it becomes a white elephant. If it is too small, an opportunity for the gain from large-scale operations has been foregone and a competitive disadvantage may have been incurred.

In buying materials and supplies in most businesses, there are almost endless opportunities to make mistakes in the decisions regarding the kind of materials to buy, the quantity to purchase, the time to buy, the source from which to buy, and the price to pay. In merchandising operations risks are involved in deciding what to make, in what quantities, and at what time. In marketing the product, the choice of the market to cultivate, the distribution channels to be utilized, the advertising to be employed, the terms on which goods are to be sold, and the prices to be charged; all these are questions to be decided, and each of these questions offers opportunities for error.

Aside from the fallibilities of judgment to which executives like other human beings are subject, the speed with which operating decisions oftentimes must be made and the incompleteness of the information which may be available enhance the likelihood of error.

Finally, it should be remembered that inaction, such as that arising from complacency or from aimless drifting, may involve risk. The complacent management is so smugly self-satisfied that it is not alert to signs of danger. Success tends to breed complacency and thus may bring about its own reversal; in a changing world danger is ever lurking around the corner, ready to trip the unwary. The management which is drifting aimlessly may not have achieved enough success to be complacent, but it also is characterized by inaction. Although it may be uneasy rather than smug, it either is unaware of the real dangers impending or it lacks the courage and the resourcefulness to steer a positive course of action. It takes a chance that luck somehow will come its way. When competitors are alert and aggressive, such chance-taking is hazardous. There is a saying in the field of sports that the team which gets the breaks usually makes them. The same is true in business. The executives who lie back inactively waiting for the breaks are likely to discover belatedly that more resourceful competitors have opened up a lead on them.

To sum up, enough evidence has been presented, I trust, to demonstrate that business management commonly operates in an environment teeming with perils and hazards.

Losses and profits

The relentless perils and hazards which abound so profusely in the business environment exact bitter penalties from those who fail to master them. The extreme penalty for inability to master these perils and hazards is bankruptcy or some analogous method of business extinction. Such purgings occur with so much frequency that for many years weekly and monthly statistics of the number and liabilities of business failures regularly have been compiled as an index of business conditions. The risk of loss through the failure of customers is so common, furthermore, that on the income statement of almost every corporation a reserve for losses from bad debts is deducted regularly and as a matter of course from the gross amount of accounts receivable. Any other procedure is not deemed to be sound accounting practice. The fact that small firms predominate in the number of business failures, moreover, does not detract from the significance of these failures as evidence of the difficulties of survival amid the hazards and perils of business operation.

When a firm fails, those who have invested their savings in the enterprise suffer a loss of capital; creditors have bad debts to write off; employees lose their jobs and their livelihood; executives suffer a loss of reputation as well as a loss of jobs and perhaps of savings; and the community in which the enterprise operated is adversely affected, particularly in instances in which the failing concern was one of the major enterprises in the community. The ramifying incidence of the penalty for nonsurvival does not lessen the bitterness of the experience.

Numerous other firms, which are partially able to meet the perils and hazards of a business existence, avoid failure or postpone it indefinitely but are chronically nonprosperous. Such firms are penalized for a lack of mastery of their hazardous environment by at least a meagerness of earnings and commonly by a gradual wasting away of capital. Such firms, moreover, serve to increase heavily the rate of business mortality in periods of crisis or depression. Having existed precariously before, they cannot survive periods of severe stress.

In view of the variety, the magnitude, and the frequent occurrence of the perils and hazards which beset business operation, it hardly is surprising that failures are so numerous or that there are so many chronic cases of nonprosperous concerns. The risk of loss is very widespread, and losses do occur with painful frequency.

Because of the difficulties of surmounting the technological, economic, social, political, and managerial risks incurred in managing a business enterprise, the question may well be raised as to why men keep on investing their efforts and their savings in such enterprises. Certainly there is no prospect that the number and magnitude of these risks will diminish, and there can be little ground for hoping that most of these risks can be dodged. Why, then, do men keep on trying to master them?

One of the main reasons why these risks are braved is the possibility of material gain in the form of profits. Fortunately there are enough successful, profitable enterprises to show that it is possible for the perils and hazards to be overcome. In some cases luck plays a part, but by and large the profitable enterprises are the ones which have been managed so as to conquer the risks instead of having been swamped by them. Profits are a reward for producing merchandise and services which consumers want, at prices which they are willing to pay, and for exercising foresight, judgment, courage, and resourcefulness in meeting the risks which inevitably are encountered. It is the task of the executive to take the lead in guiding those who are associated with him in the enterprise so that, if possible, the assets entrusted to them will be utilized profitably and with sustained prosperity.

The very challenge presented by the perils and hazards encountered in business management also constitutes a reason as to why men continue to take the risk, even against large odds. It would be far too extravagant to say that man typically is a risk-taking animal, because obviously there are many men who shun risk-taking. Nevertheless, there are still enough willing risk-takers to keep the spark of progress alive. In business, as in various other human activities, the risk-takers make possible much of the ease and comfort enjoyed by those who shun the risky life.

The mirages of security

In a world in which plans and hopes and lives are upset so frequently by changing conditions it is not surprising that there should be incessant demands for security — security of jobs, security of income, security of capital, and security against disturbance of habitual ways of living and of doing business. The fear of insecurity has been accentuated by the events of the last half century. Business depressions and red-tinged criticisms have shaken faith in our economic system. Two world wars have thrown the political systems of the world into turmoil in addition to causing economic and social upheavals. And technological and other changes have come apace. The fear of insecurity generated by these experiences has intensified the desire for security.

Concretely, the demands for security have manifested themselves in numerous ways. Some of the labor legislation enacted and some of the practices of labor unions have been aimed primarily toward assuring job security for workmen and also to provide security of income. The demands by some of the union leaders for a guaranteed annual wage are another specific example of efforts to attain security.

In the investment field large pools of savings are held by institutions which have been impelled either by law or by custom to seek "secure" investments. The insurance companies, the savings banks, the financial managers of endowed institutions, and the holders of many trust funds either have been compelled by law or have had plausible reasons as to why the funds which they hold should not be invested in any form which involves risk. Largely as a result of the workings of the tax system applied in this country during recent years, these pools of funds available only for riskless investment have come to constitute a rather substantial portion of the total investable funds. Capital, as well as labor, has been seeking security.

For business, legislation has been sought on various subjects with security as the objective. The tariff has long been a controversial subject of security legislation. Laws such as the Miller-Tydings Act, permitting control of resale prices by manufacturers of branded merchandise, and the Robinson-Patman Act, nominally an antitrust measure, are examples of legislation enacted at the behest of business groups who were seeking to attain security for themselves.

Then there was NRA, with its blue eagle, a scheme to protect business against "chiselers" and other allegedly unfair practitioners. When NRA was set up in 1933, it was widely hailed by depression-distraught businessmen as a means of salvation, that is, as an assurance of security. Although NRA has long since been dead, there is still a yearning for that type of government-sponsored security, I judge, latent in some business breasts.

So far as I am aware, I was the first person to make a public statement criticizing NRA, and I still recall rather vividly the vibrancy of that atmosphere. NRA, with its elaborate codes of business conduct and price-policing provisions, went into effect in the spring of 1933. In September of that year I was invited to speak at a meeting of cost accountants in Boston, and I chose to state my conviction that such industrial police measures as those of NRA were not in the true public interest and that unless they were abrogated they eventually would lead business into a strait jacket where initiative would be deadened and progress stifled. I recognized that undesirable practices did exist, and I sympathized with those who had suffered heavy losses during the depression just ending. But the cure seemed to me to be worse than the ailment. After the meeting was adjourned, several members of the audience came to me to tell me very quietly that they agreed with my views.

About six weeks later, by invitation, I spoke at a large "national recovery" meeting in New York City. Before accepting the invitation I had warned the chairman of the committee of arrangements that I probably would present a discordant view, but after several days of deliberation the committee decided to make the invitation firm, with the understanding that I should be entirely free to express my views, whatever they were. All the other speakers at the meeting, including the United States Secretary of Commerce, eulogized NRA. I stated my dissent with considerable emphasis. At the conclusion of the meeting I received several quiet statements of approbation.

To me the most significant aspect of this episode, however, was the number of instances during the next few weeks in which people asked me how I dared to make a speech so critical of a popular government policy. These questioners obviously were gravely apprehensive that it was personally dangerous for anyone to speak freely on such matters. At this distance it is difficult to comprehend the awe and fear which then was prevalent.

During the next few years I saw fit to speak and write critically of several other government policies, such as the devaluation of the dollar, for example. Shortly after some of these criticisms had been given publicity, by what was presumably an odd coincidence, I received a summons from the Collector of Internal Revenue to present myself at his office in Boston, with all my records, for an examination of my income-tax report for the preceding year. After waiting about half an hour beyond the appointed time, I was ushered to the desk of an examiner, a thickset, ruddy-faced gentleman, who had the air of an ex-prize fighter. He brusquely asked my name, reached into his desk for a folder, and then asked me: "Are you married?" To which I replied, "Yes." "When were you married?" I told him. "Where were you married?" I told him. "That's all," he said, and the examination was over without any reference to the income-tax report itself. No reason was given as to why my marital status was questioned, and although I would have liked to ask what occasioned such attention, I discreetly refrained. For several years thereafter I was called upon annually for an examination of my income-tax reports, but all the other examiners were polite and courteous.

In the agricultural field the counterpart of NRA undertook to provide security for the farmers by killing off little pigs and by other valorization schemes. So many tender hearts were hurt by the mass execution of the little pigs that public sentiment did not permit its repetition. Thereafter little pigs were permitted to grow into big hogs which could be slaughtered for the market in regular course without objection, and prices were supported by other means.

Succeeding generations of little pigs were spared, but measures for valorizing other agricultural products continued to evolve, until in 1950 the government has acquired vast stocks of corn, wheat, cotton, potatoes, and many other products merely to provide price protection for the farmers.

The foregoing statements cover by no means all the attempts that are being made to secure insulation against the raw vicissitudes of a changing environment. Enough instances have been cited, however, to indicate the nature of the protective measures sought and to suggest their significance to business management.

The bulk of these visions of security, unfortunately, are but mirages. That is a cruel conclusion, perhaps, but I have never found merit in trying to dodge the truth, however unwelcome it may be.

The forces which are causing changes to occur are too irresistible to be stopped by most of these security measures. When the automobile became popular and the markets for buggies and horseshoes and numerous other items declined, the jobs of men making those products were gone. Other jobs were appearing in Detroit, to be sure, but there was no security for the buggy-maker in Amesbury. When the Waltham Watch Company failed to keep pace with changes in its industry, there could be no job security for its employees. Competitors developed new watch designs which gained greater consumer acceptance than was enjoyed by the merely reliable Waltham timepieces. Those competitors also utilized new methods of sales promotion and equipped their plants with modernized machinery not matched by the Waltham company. In the face of such conditions, the customary methods of seeking job security were merely another mirage.

John L. Lewis, president of the United Mine Workers, understandably is seeking greater job security and income security for the coal miners. But the very success of some of his efforts tends to cause greater insecurity. Uncertainty of supply, as a result of frequent strikes, and rising prices, brought about by higher costs, are impelling enough consumers and industrial users of coal to shift to other fuels and other sources of power to imperil the market for coal. As demand falls off, there is less work for the miners. If daily wages are raised to offset the loss of work, some of the mines will either have to raise their prices, and thus discourage demand still more, or close down. Mr. Lewis and others seeking security by such measures are chasing mirages.

Security of investments also may be mirage. Temporary

security may be attained, of course, for some indefinite volume of investments, but universal security can be only a mirage. Changes in technological processes which render equipment obsolete, shifts in demand, the development of new methods of conducting business, and changes in economic, social, and political conditions, all these occasion inescapable risk to investors. Whether the capital is represented by pieces of paper marked "stock" or by pieces of paper marked "bond," the real capital — the machinery, the inventory, the accounts receivable — is subject to the perils and hazards of a changing environment and losses will occur. Risk-taking is essential to a dynamic, healthy, growing economy, and pursuit of security of investment on a large scale inherently implies a timid, defeatist attitude.

Security of investment in terms of buying power also is an illusion. This has been proved over and over again in centuries of experience. But it is not necessary to go further back than the last decade to find an illustration. During the Second World War, when billions of dollars were obtained from the public by the sale of government bonds, the "security" of the savings thus invested was stressed. The fiscal policies pursued by the government, however, have led to a price inflation, with the result that those savings have lost at least one half of their original buying power. The bondholders have a safe investment in that they will receive back eventually the same number of dollars that they paid for the bonds, plus interest, but what the dollars will buy when the bonds mature no one knows. Until we can stop wars, end nationalism, prevent new inventions, and end various other types of change, stability of prices is a fantasy.

Legislation designed to provide security for small businessmen also is illusory in numerous instances. New enterprises capable of vigorous growth are essential to a healthy economy, and such enterprises can be aided by the elimination of handicaps such as those imposed by some of our tax laws. But much of the small-business legislation is aimed at bolstering up small concerns which lack the managerial ability and the stamina to exist in a rough world of change. In view of the relentless nature of the changes constantly taking place in the environment, indiscriminate attempts to aid "small business" are certain to be abortive. An enterprise, large or small, operated by a man who lacks managerial sagacity, cannot be made successful merely by the infusion of government credit or by other political stimuli.

The attainment of price security through valorization schemes is still another illusion. In May 1933, in a research report, after reviewing a comprehensive series of government price-support programs in this country and in foreign countries, I stated: "The world, in modern times of peace, probably has never witnessed such a series of experiments at price control as these valorization schemes have constituted. White, yellow, and brown races, North Americans, South Americans, Europeans, and Asiatics, in desperation, all have tried their hand at this experimenting. The plans have varied in form, scope, and timing. The one outstanding feature that they have had in common is that all have failed." [1] My subsequent studies[2] of raw commodity prices did not lead me to change that conclusion.

There is one exception, however, to that general conclusion, and the reason for its success underscores one of the main causes for the illusoriness of other valorization schemes. The exception is silver. Since 1878 the United States government, under political pressure from the silver-producing

[1] Melvin T. Copeland, *Raw Material Prices and Business Conditions* (Boston: Division of Research, Harvard Business School, 1933), p. 47.

[2] The chief of these is *A Raw Commodity Revolution* (Boston: Division of Research, Harvard Business School, 1938).

states, has maintained an artificial, stable market for silver, at a substantial cost to the taxpayers, of course. That valorization scheme has worked merely because silver is produced chiefly as a by-product in the mining of other nonferrous metals. Because of its by-product character, the artificially high price for silver has not caused production of the metal to increase to a breakdown point.

In contrast to the silver experience, take potatoes, currently a hot political problem. As a condition for government price support, the potato farmers were directed to restrict the acreage planted to that crop. But by planting the rows closer together, using more fertilizer per acre, and applying more insecticide, the farmers produced so many potatoes in 1949 that the government was almost swamped with them. The situation is similarly embarrassing for numerous other crops for which prices are supported by the government.

Without complete and rigid control of production, any government price-support plan is doomed to ultimate failure. Continued pursuit of this mirage of price security through government support can lead only to bitter disillusionment. One possible outcome of such valorization schemes is devastating monetary inflation, brought on by the deficits in the federal budget caused by expenditures for price supports. The alternative to such inflation is the adoption of control measures characteristic of a police state. Any dream of a middle ground is an illusion.

All these illusions about the possibilities of attaining security in a perilous and hazardous environment obviously affect business management directly or indirectly. It is incumbent on an executive leader to recognize the illusions and to see through them. It also is incumbent on him to accept the challenge of seeking constructive means, so far as it is within his power, for meeting the conditions which give rise to the illusions.

The spirit of mastery

Man can rise above his environment and master it. That is what man has been doing for ages. That is the history of the human race. And man's achievements in rising above his environment have resulted from a will to succeed, from a rugged spirit of mastery. That will to succeed, that rugged spirit of mastery, has been characteristic of leaders in business administration as well as of leaders in other human activities.

The geographical frontier, which for three centuries exerted such a significant influence on American life and institutions, was mastered through the indomitable will and resourcefulness of the pioneers. The geographical frontier now is gone, but the environment in which we seek to exist presents hazards and perils hardly less challenging than those mastered by our forefathers. Indians and wolves no longer are lurking in the shadows, but other types of "varmint" have taken their places.

In mastering the hazardous business environment, the will to succeed has necessitated the exercise of foresight, imagination, and resourcefulness. It has called for courage and steady nerves and a zest for adventure. The opportunities for exercising these qualities are no less today than they have been in the past.

In order to exercise foresight, the first requirement is an attitude of accepting the probability of change as a normal expectation. Once the probability of changing conditions is accepted as a normal prospect, the first steps toward preparedness can be taken. When the likelihood of change is appreciated, then by observing the forces at work, both internal forces in the individual business and external forces, trends can be observed, new developments noted, and the rate of acceleration of the various forces judged. The better the forces at work are gauged, the more intelligently can preparations be made for meeting such new situations as may eventuate. The environment must be understood before it can be mastered.

Resourcefulness for meeting the hazards and perils of the business environment manifests itself, of course, in many forms, such as the maintenance of financial flexibility and adequate financial reserves, the modernization of plant equipment, the revamping of production methods, the development of new products, the cultivation of new markets, and the adaptation of the organization to the changing conditions. The choice of the steps to be taken in each particular case depends on the estimate of the situation. There is no single, simple formula for solving all these problems of adaptation. In estimating the situation and choosing the course of action to be followed under dynamic circumstances, imagination and courage are called for. Courage and steady nerves also are commonly needed in following that course of action through the vicissitudes of uncertainty to a successful culmination. That is a manifestation of the spirit of mastery.

The ability of their executives to exercise foresight and resourcefulness and to master perplexing situations has been a major factor in the growth and prosperity of numerous large corporations. Large size in itself, however, is not assurance that a corporation will employ executives with the ability to master the environment in which they operate — witness some of the big, clumsy enterprises in which executive leadership of a high caliber is patently lacking.

The ability to deal constructively and effectively with the hazardous environment in which they are conducted is not confined, furthermore, to large companies. In fact, a small enterprise with executives who are resourceful and courageous often can more than hold its own with large competitors. The very forces which are constantly causing changes to occur in the business environment afford some of the greatest opportunities for new enterprises to enter the business field. As new methods develop and as shifts in demand occur, chances are offered for alert and nimble small-scale operators to gain a foothold. If they have executive ability and a determination to survive, they may become the large enterprises of the future. So long as the environment continues to undergo change and so long as a genuine spirit of risk-taking survives, the door to progress and prosperity will not be closed. Our business environment is full of hazards and perils, but those very dangers also afford opportunities for achieving new strength.

The competent executive cannot afford to dream of featherbeds and security. His task is to master the perils and hazards of an ever changing world.

VIII

Timing

In baseball a great batter has a highly developed sense of timing. He learns to time his swing to meet the ball at just the right instant for applying his maximum power. In other sports — football, hockey, rowing, and golf, for example — keen timing likewise is characteristic of outstanding performers. And in business management maximum effectiveness also is attained when executive action is keenly timed. In meeting the perils and hazards of an ever changing environment, proficiency in timing is a particularly valuable administrative asset.

The art of timing

Timing is an art. Although proficiency in timing unquestionably can be improved by study and practice, I suspect that a sense of timing at least comes close to being an innate quality. Business executives who are especially proficient in timing seem typically to time their actions almost intuitively. Other executives who are less proficient either neglect the time factor or are virtually unaware of its existence.

In most business decisions timing is an element; there is a question not only as to what to do but also as to when to do it; and nicety in timing is a deft achievement. In bringing out a new product, for example, the decision involves consideration of such factors as the demand for established products, the manufacturing capacity available, the company's financial resources, and the competitive situation. One company, for instance, had perfected a new product which was ready for the market in 1943. The company had ample financial resources, and it could have put the new item into production immediately, at least in a limited way, despite the fact that its plants were then operating at capacity. Under the circumstances the executives decided to wait until after the end of the war to launch the new item, and by that decision an opportunity was lost. In 1944 a competitor put a product on the market almost identical with the one being held in abeyance by the first company. The first company thereupon reversed its decision and offered its new product for sale, but it had missed its opportunity to gain a head start. The competitor's timing was shrewder, and the competitor thereby gained a marketing advantage and acquired prestige which the first company has not yet been able to match.

During the 1920's while General Motors was developing the Chevrolet car for the low-price field and adding style to its appearance, Mr. Ford persisted in manufacturing his standardized Model T. By making over a million cars a year of that one model, Mr. Ford kept his costs and his prices low. In 1927, however, Ford's sales dropped about sixty per cent and the sales of Chevrolets ran far ahead of those of Fords. Belatedly Mr. Ford scrambled to put out a new model of more stylish appearance. His persistence in refusing to introduce new models until a drastic drop in sales forced such action enabled Chevrolet to become firmly established as a large-scale producer of low-price cars. It also facilitated the entrance of other cars, such as Plymouth, into that market. Mr. Ford had great genius for production but not for timing market trends.

At about the same time that these major developments

were occurring in the automobile industry, a revolution took place also in the moving-picture industry. During the early 1920's Western Electric Company had been experimenting with devices for reproducing sound in motion pictures. By the fall of 1924, sound pictures were a laboratory success.[1] Western Electric Company attempted to interest each of the more important moving-picture producers in the new device but met with no welcome. The use of the new device would have necessitated changes in production techniques and might therefore have been costly. The large producers, furthermore, had heavy investments in moving-picture theaters, and use of the new sound device would have necessitated replacing expensive reproducing and projecting equipment in the theaters. Consequently, the large producers chose not to try out the innovation.

In 1925, however, Warner Brothers Pictures, Inc., then a relatively small producer with no heavy investment in theaters, became interested in the Western Electric Company's new technique. Experiments were carried on, and in August 1926 a Warner picture was shown in New York with synchronized musical accompaniment. On October 6, 1927, another Warner picture, *The Jazz Singer,* starring Al Jolson, opened on Broadway. In that picture a few words were spoken. That demonstration that the human voice as well as music could be transmitted by the sound-reproducing device created such a sensation that other producers rushed all at once to turn out talking pictures. Warner Brothers, however, had such a head start with that technique that it enjoyed a strategic advantage on which it capitalized to become a large producer. By gaining a time advantage a small and rather obscure company had jumped into effective competition with the former leaders. In many another industry an

[1] Fitzhugh Green, *The Film Finds Its Tongue* (New York: Putnam, 1929), p. 43.

agile, young enterprise has taken the play away from larger, well-entrenched competitors whose success has made them stodgy.

In the tin-plate business radical technological changes took place in the decade beginning in 1929; the continuous cold-rolling process and various other new manufacturing methods were introduced, and several companies substantially increased their tin-plate producing capacity. The MacKeesport Tinplate Company, however, delayed modernizing its plant. New developments were taking place rapidly and obsolescence was high. The company was operating profitably with its old equipment, and its executives apparently hesitated to make radical changes. As a result of that procrastination the company fell so far behind the procession that in 1940 it was liquidated.

As these illustrations indicate, time cannot safely be flouted.

The question of *when* to build a new plant often is a major problem in timing. Consideration of that question requires that attention be given to many factors, such as potential sales, available labor supply, raw material situation, managerial crew, financial resources, and so on. Furthermore, since a new plant represents a long-term capital investment, the cost of construction is a factor of major significance, and the cost of construction is substantially affected by general business conditions. The timing of the building of a new plant with reference to general business conditions thus puts executive judgment to a severe test. If a new plant is built at about the peak of a boom period, as frequently has been the case in the past, it is likely to be a white elephant. On the other hand, great courage as well as foresighted husbanding of resources is required for embarking on the construction of a new plant when business is slack and the outlook bleak, but such a move may be a most timely one.

Changes in key personnel commonly present problems in

timing. When a new man has been appointed to a responsible administrative position, how long shall he be given to demonstrate his capacity to handle the job? If he fails to measure up, how long before severance takes place? If a once competent member of the administrative force starts to slip, how long is he to be permitted to retain his position? These are particularly difficult problems in timing, because of the emotional conflicts and human relationships involved. This much is certain, however: delay after a certain point increases the difficulty of handling such situations satisfactorily.

This problem of timing changes in personnel is particularly troublesome in an educational institution. A man who has been appointed to a faculty always has some qualifications and some supporters. Even if he does not live up to his early promise, he will have made friends who are disposed to overlook his shortcomings and to excuse his deficiencies. Not uncommonly he is a personable individual, and for some of his associates his deficiencies in teaching ability or in scholarly attainments are covered up by his attractive personality. Consequently it happens with some frequency that there are strong pressures to have such a man retained and even promoted. If he is retained, it may become more difficult for him later to obtain a position elsewhere, and then sympathy comes in to exert pressure for retaining him still longer. In educational institutions, as in business, after a man has had a fair trial and has failed to show full competency to handle his position, the time has come to sever connections. Dilatory action can be only harmful to the institution or the business concern. The retention of one noncompetent individual almost invariably leads to the retention of other noncompetents and thus brings about a deterioration in the quality of the whole enterprise.

Marketing is another managerial area to which the art of timing is conspicuously applicable. An example of the strategic timing of a change in distribution policy is afforded by a company manufacturing a bulky consumer product. Before the Second World War the company had been following a rather nondescript catch-as-catch-can policy of distribution. During the war years, the company's facilities were utilized almost completely for the production of military supplies. After V-J Day the executives decided to put into effect a policy of selected distribution, that is, to seek distribution of its product only through carefully selected retail stores each of which would carry an adequate inventory and utilize effective promotional methods. Inasmuch as there was a large backlog of accumulated demand for such products and established relations with most retailers had perforce been suspended by the company while it was engaged on war production, an exceptional opportunity was afforded the company to make a radical change in distribution policy with a minimum of risk.

The chief competitors of the company just referred to were unprepared for any such change. They drifted along watchfully waiting to observe whether the new policy worked out well for the company which had adopted it. Five years later they were still drifting. If the policy proves to be successful, as it gives every evidence of doing, the competitors will have lost time which perhaps can never be made up, and it also is improbable that they now can make a corresponding change in policy without a temporary disruption of their sales. As competition becomes sharper, they will hesitate to risk disrupting their markets even temporarily. Meanwhile the company which changed its policy at the opportune time is sailing smoothly ahead. It took real courage to decide on the policy chosen in 1945, but the timing was opportune and the stakes were high enough to justify the taking of the risk.

Advertising executives of necessity are particularly alert to the art of timing. The essential ingredients of an effective advertising program include not only appealing design and well-drafted copy, but also strategic timing to capitalize on potential demand and to gain competitive advantage. In order to attain maximum effectiveness, the right date has to be chosen for opening the campaign and for each successive step in the program.

In style merchandising the art of timing goes hand in hand with the art of design. The style leaders time the introduction of new fashions to catch the fancy of buyers who want something new, something distinctive, something to replace merchandise which is becoming outmoded. Fashion is essentially paradoxical. To be successful a fashion must be accepted by those whose choice will be imitated. The more successful a fashion is, the more widely it will be copied. And the more widely it is copied, the sooner it becomes outmoded.

The manufacturers who produce style merchandise for the mass market are not style leaders; they are copiers. They must wait until a new fashion has come into vogue before they successfully can add that fashion to their lines. If they were to offer the same merchandise a few months before the fashion came into vogue, they could not sell it, and the fact that they had offered it would deter the style leaders from starting that particular fashion. The mass producers must time their entry into the market with a particular fashion to follow rather than to anticipate the style leaders.

From an administrative standpoint style merchandising calls for rapid adjustment to continual and frequent changes in demand. Designing, purchasing, production, pricing, and sales have to be adjusted quickly to each change in a volatile market, and the various activities are so closely interdependent that they must all be adjusted almost simultaneously. Under these circumstances the activities of an enterprise manufacturing style merchandise are not sufficiently standardized or stable to permit the delegation of much decision-making to lieutenants. Hence, the small manufacturer who can constantly feel the pulse of the market and who can transmit his instructions directly and immediately to the operating forces is in a strategic competitive position. In such an industry the advantages of quick decision-making and speedy transmittal of decisions to operatives more than offset the economies which might otherwise be gained from large-scale manufacturing.

The executive of a large cotton manufacturing company which makes gray cloth and also operates a converting plant for finishing the fabric has told me on various occasions that his company is at a disadvantage in competition with small merchant converters on style goods. As he puts it: "The small converter can turn around much more quickly than we can." That is his method of explaining that the proprietor of a small converting business, operating with a few assistants, can make decisions more quickly and therefore more effectively than similarly comprehensive decisions can be made in a large organization where approval of several department heads has to be obtained before the final verdict is rendered. The predominance of small concerns in the style industries is attributable in considerable measure to the advantages which they enjoy in administrative timing.

As the variety of examples cited indicates, the problems of timing are well-nigh universal, and the decision-making process almost inevitably involves the art of timing. If decisions are made too far in advance or moves are made too early, the mistakes may be costly. On the other hand, if action is tardy the delay may be disastrous. Mastery of the art of timing contributes substantially to executive achievement.

Time spans

The span of time within which effective action can be taken varies according to the strength of the forces at work and their velocities. On one of the tests used by the Army in selecting personnel for certain tasks in 1918, I have been told, the following question was included: "Suppose you were driving a truck and, as you came around a sharp curve at sixty miles an hour, you saw another truck close at hand coming at you head on at the same speed, what would you do?" To which one candidate is reported to have replied: "I'd take my truck apart and hide it in the bushes." I cannot vouch for the authenticity of this anecdote, but I do know that in business administration conflicting forces moving at high velocities not infrequently are encountered, with no bushes handy for refuge.

In the summer of 1931 the executives of a well-known corporation faced a critical price problem. The company's production was highly seasonal and a large inventory was on hand. The market was weak and competitors were shading prices to move their stocks. The president of this company was fully aware of the competitive situation, but he was reluctant to make a sharp reduction in price. He was convinced that his company was a low-cost producer and that therefore it had an advantage over the competitors. Consequently he negotiated a short-term bank loan to enable the company to carry its inventory while waiting for its high-cost competitors to be forced to curtail operations.

The market continued to drop and eventually that company had to dispose of its inventory at a much greater loss than would have been incurred in reducing prices sufficiently to move its inventory in 1931. This executive made a common mistake of underestimating the velocity of the influences forcing prices down and of overestimating the speed with which a low-cost advantage can be made effective. Over a long span of time cost is a major factor in determining price, but for a short period cost often has very little effect on price determination. In this instance the forces which were depressing the market were so powerful that the price fell far below the cost of even the low-cost producer. Nevertheless the other producers had sufficient capital resources to weather the emergency and were not forced to cease operations.

This is but one of several instances which I have encountered where there has been a failure to reckon realistically with the span of time required for disposing of high-cost competitors.

A mastery of the art of timing comprehends an ability to sense the time span available for preparation for action, or the span within which action has to be taken to attain its maximum effectiveness. The length of the span varies with every situation. In some cases plenty of time is available for working out plans and putting them into effect. In many other cases the executive and his staff have to "work against time," that is, the span is so uncomfortably limited that preparations have to be compressed into a short period, and short cuts have to be taken wherever possible. In extreme cases the action takes on an emergency character. In each case the executive has to decide whether "to keep his shirt on" or to go into action rapidly.

Part of the art of timing lies in an executive's ability to read the handwriting on the wall or otherwise to sense an impending change well in advance of the point where it mounts to full force. The executive who has such a knack usually enjoys a relatively long time span within which to prepare for dealing with a new situation. Competitors who awaken belatedly to the problem obviously have shorter time spans within which to act and therefore must hurry and press in their preparations. Variations in executive astuteness thus cause differences in the effective time span for directly competing concerns.

As many of the examples cited in preceding sections have

indicated, competition frequently is a major factor in determining the length of a time span. A competitive advantage can be gained by winning a head start in introducing a new product, for example, or in adopting an improved method of doing business. Conversely, a competitor who seldom exercises initiative but rather follows the moves made by others is likely to fall further and further behind in the race. The fellow who habitually has to engage in a stern chase typically has a short time span within which to act. His moves are rushed and therefore less well prepared. And he has less freedom of action. Incidentally, it may not be amiss to point out that timing is one of many vital aspects of competition generally neglected by economic theorists.

Research is a type of activity in which the time span usually is a factor of major concern. This is true of technical research and also of business research. The researcher typically wishes to proceed at his own pace and sometimes, in his zest for pursuing a new discovery or for polishing off a bit of new knowledge, he becomes quite oblivious to the passage of time. He may even resent any reference to a time limit. On the other hand, few research budgets are unlimited and budgetary considerations therefore commonly make it necessary at some stage to wind up a project, even if thereby the researcher's happiness is disturbed. The research administrator is continually involved in this conflict between the researchers' desires and the hard facts of a budget.

In business research another complication is the fact that so many business executives have little appreciation of the time required for the gathering of facts and for their analysis and interpretation. Business executives frequently have urged our research organization to undertake projects where the time spans would have been too short to permit the making of more than slapdash surveys. In some instances this urgency has resulted from a belated awakening to the need for objective studies of new problems. In other instances the urgency has arisen out of an impatient lack of comprehension. One outstanding example of the latter type was the chief executive of a large and highly successful company who was an engineer by training. He had demonstrated infinite patience in the development of the company's program of technical research. Whereas he readily would approve a long-range technical research project, he expected it to be possible to have a complicated business research project completed within a year. He had no real perspective on the time span for business research, a shortcoming which is shared by numerous other technically trained executives.

The time required for securing the acceptance of a new idea was demonstrated by one of my early experiences in research, although I did not appreciate it until some years later. One of my early research assignments was to organize and supervise a study of operating expenses in retail grocery stores. The first results of that study were published in November 1915. Shortly thereafter I spoke, by invitation, at a regional meeting of wholesale grocers in Reading, Pennsylvania. I explained our research program and urged the wholesalers to encourage their customers — the retail grocers — to keep adequate accounts so that they might know their costs and that they might be able to coöperate in our research program. By comparing his operating figures, on a percentage basis, with the standards developed by the research, it was hoped that each grocer might learn how to operate his own business more efficiently. In my talk to the wholesale grocers, I stressed their responsibility for helping their customers to become better merchants and thereby strengthen themselves for meeting the growing chain-store competition.

The report of the meeting in the New York *Journal of Commerce* the following morning bore the caption: "Is the Jobber his Brother's Keeper?" That caption referred to my talk. At the time I naïvely assumed that the caption was a pleasantry of the jovial grocery editor of the *Journal of Commerce.*

About ten years later, when competition from chain stores was decimating the ranks of the independent grocers and their suppliers, the wholesalers, the monthly publication of the National Wholesale Grocers Association began to feature articles on how certain wholesalers were undertaking to bolster their customers by inducing them to keep better accounts. I had nothing to do with this later development because my evangelistic career in the grocery trade had been cut short by the First World War and by the subsequent pressure of other research and teaching assignments. At the later date, however, it became apparent that the caption on the report of my Reading talk was not a pleasantry but an echo of a voice from the academic wilderness. Had that novel idea been made to register in 1915, more retail and wholesale grocers might have survived. Ten years later, however, their effective time span had become desperately short.

Time is an asset which one cannot lightly afford to waste. Other assets may be replenished or substitutes may be found to fill their places. There is no substitute for wasted time.

Foresight and insight

As has been stated, timing is an art. And the more proficiently this art is exercised, the less conspicuous it becomes. When an executive foresees trouble brewing, because of changing conditions or from other causes, and takes steps forehandedly to meet the situation, a readjustment oftentimes is carried through so smoothly and so unostentatiously that it attracts little attention and is appreciated only by connoisseurs of administration.

Foresight in anticipating administrative problems provides a longer time for action and thereby not only permits more careful preparation but also allows greater freedom of action.

Conversely, a lack of foresight leads to handicaps. A company, for example, which does not recognize adverse trends or which drifts aimlessly in the hope that emergency trends will not prove to be serious loses more and more of its freedom of action as the situation deteriorates. If financial losses occur and working capital is depleted, for instance, the company presently finds itself in a situation where it does not have the funds for developing a major new program for rehabilitation, and its record by that time may well be such as to deter investors from providing new funds, except perhaps on onerous terms. Foresight becomes conspicuous through its absence, and the greater the lack of foresight, the less the freedom in timing one's action.

Executives of the type prone to "go off half-cocked" and those who thrive on emergencies are notably lacking in foresight, even though in some instances I have observed they pride themselves on being foresighted. Those types of executives never "have enough time" to produce well-devised, strategically timed programs. The executive who is prone to go off half-cocked continually has to be bailed out of his difficulties by other members of the organization, not always an easy task and never a welcome one. The executive who thrives on emergencies, who subconsciously dotes on them, also constitutes a problem for his associates. He not only "keeps them on their toes" but he also frays their nerves and even may cause some of them to develop stomach ulcers, by proxy as it were.

By permitting greater freedom of action, which is another way of phrasing better timing, the exercise of foresight helps to make possible a smoothly running organization. By lessening the wear and tear on the human machinery of administration, foresight facilitates constructive management.

Effective timing, however, calls not only for foresight, in

so far as that is humanly possible of attainment, but also for insight. During the Battle of the Bulge in the Ardennes in January 1945, General Montgomery is reported to have said wistfully, and quite significantly, that he would like to get inside General von Rundstedt's head for a couple of minutes. Insight of that sort also is invaluable in business administration. The executive who can get inside the head of his chief competitor gains a great advantage in timing his own operations. To the extent that he can read the minds of leading suppliers, large customers, and labor union officials, an executive obviously can time his own actions more strategically. Insight is not a matter of cold logic. Real insight is an attainment which includes an understanding of temperaments, emotions, courage, resourcefulness, and other attributes as well as an observation of habitual courses of action and a comprehension of strategic reasoning.

Insight itself is in part a product of time — time for observation. While General Montgomery was contending with General Rommel in North Africa, he did learn how Rommel's mind worked. Over a period of time by observation he gained insight as to what Rommel was likely to do in a particular situation and when he was likely to do it. In business affairs likewise an executive with an aptitude for insight learns by observation how to get inside the heads of competitors, suppliers, and customers. If he is in the sugar industry, he learns how the executives of each of his major competitors are likely to react to a reduction in price, to an invasion of their sales territories, or to a new program of sales promotion. In the automobile industry or in the textile industry, the reactions would differ from those in the sugar industry. In fact, each industry has its own special conditions, its own traditions, and its own personalities, sometimes even its own peculiar personalities. In each of those industries, however, some executives do learn by observation and experience how to get inside the minds of their competitors and thus to time their strategy advantageously.

It is not yet illegal to exercise insight for competitive purposes, but some of the current theories well may lead to its being outlawed. The theory of "conscious parallel action," promulgated by the Federal Trade Commission in the Rigid Steel Conduit case, comes close to charging a man with being guilty of collusion if he reads the mind of a competitor and is guided by what he thereby discovers.

In recent years labor unions have confronted many business executives with baffling new problems. Somewhat belatedly those executives now are beginning to seek an understanding of what goes on in the heads of the union officials. Such insight is of much greater significance than laws and rules and regulations.

In business administration generally insight facilitates strategic timing. And both foresight and insight are essential to the art of timing.

A good sense of timing is peculiarly a qualification for executive leadership. The chief executive necessarily takes a leading part in the making of major decisions and in planning the arrangements for having them combined in harmonious action. In any organization, teamwork, of course, is a much to be desired attainment. Teamwork requires a choice of competent men to serve on the team, proper instruction and intelligent coaching of the members of the team, a mutual understanding of the over-all objectives of the enterprise, a spirit of coöperation, and not least a pulling together when the team goes into action. Pulling together is achieved by a nicety in timing under masterly leadership.

In an earlier chapter the question was raised as to what there is left for an executive to do once he has a competent lieutenant in each key position. Since that question was raised, numerous tasks for the executive have been pointed out, and here the task of demonstrating leadership in timing group efforts to attain the maximum teamwork is added to the list. The effective leader symphonizes the efforts of the members of the organization so that each performs his task at the right moment to produce a maximum over-all effectiveness.

IX

Nurturing Morale

The A Manufacturing Company, located in a large midwestern city, has a notable reputation as being a good place to work. If a visitor talks with people around town, he learns that jobs with the A company are highly prized. There are numerous persons working for other companies in the city who would have preferred to take jobs with the A company, had positions there been available when they were seeking new employment. If the visitor drives out to the plant in a taxicab, he finds that the driver manifests a local pride in the A company even though he has no connection with it. The driver has no doubts about its being a good place to work. If the visitor has an opportunity to become acquainted with members of the organization and with employees in the various departments of the company, he finds that they are unusually loyal to the company and that they are zealous for its continued prosperity. Their loyalty and zeal transcend mere self-interest. They look to the welfare of the whole company. In other words, morale in the A company is high.

There are other companies in the United States, of course, where morale is as high as in the A company, but there also are numerous others which do not rank so high in morale, some even in which indifference and discontent are prevalent.

The work climate

Why is one company looked upon by its employees and by many other people in the community as being a good place to work whereas in neighboring plants of other companies the employees look upon their jobs merely as meal tickets? That question poses a major test of executive leadership.

The answer to that question is not to be found solely by an examination of the physical and economic environments of the business. A dirty, ill-kept plant, for example, may breed unrest among the employees, but in a clean plant, with up-to-date equipment, unrest and discontent also may appear. In the latter case the executives of the company may even feel disappointed and hurt when they discover that the excellent physical equipment and attractive physical surroundings which they have provided do not in themselves produce loyalty and enthusiasm among the employees. An attractive physical environment for work certainly has its merits, but physical conditions are only one factor and not necessarily the chief factor in determining the morale of the workers.

Likewise a low wage scale may be a cause for discontent among the workers, but a high wage scale does not necessarily assure high morale. Loyalty and a zealousness for the success of the enterprise are not produced merely by dollars and cents. If other conditions are favorable, a relatively high wage scale naturally makes employment attractive, but the other conditions cannot be ignored.

Among these other conditions, human relations loom large. In uncovering the human aspects of the work climate, the pioneer research studies by Elton Mayo, Fritz Roethlisberger and their associates have been particularly valuable.[1] Those

[1] A complete list of the publications by this group, 1926–1945, is appended in Dr. Elton Mayo's outstanding volume on *The Social Problems of an Industrial Civilization* (Boston, Division of Research, Harvard Business School, 1945).

studies are sufficiently well known so that I assume that it is not necessary for me to undertake any summarizing of them here. Instead I will refer to certain other experiences which also illustrate the human aspects of the work climate.

A recent study, previously referred to, which in fact is an outgrowth of the Mayo, Roethlisberger series, by Messrs. Ulrich, Booz, and Lawrence of the research staff of the Harvard Business School, describes the conditions faced by a new general manager of a branch plant operated by a large corporation with headquarters in New York City. This plant, one of a number operated by the company, employed about five hundred persons. The industry in which the company carried on its business was young and technological changes occurred with rapidity. The research group stated:

> One of the most important problems the new manager inherited was the lack of teamwork among the various departments. Production men often failed to notify production control when manufacturing difficulties caused them to alter plans. Production control men made sudden changes in manufacturing schedules that embarrassed the men in purchasing. Salesmen made commitments that the production men could not fulfill. Work-in-process inventory grew alarmingly on the accountants' books, but actual count was far below the book figure. The engineering department sent projects to production which production men were unable to make and in which engineers had lost interest. Engineers sought the right to buy their own specialized equipment without notifying the purchasing department. Engineers, considering themselves the elite of the plant, were at odds with other departments. Most of the plant personnel seemed to have a frightened attitude.
>
> Within the factory, a personnel program embodying such features as a suggestion system and a pension plan was in operation. The effect of this program on employee morale was negligible, however, since it was offset by the daily events that filled the foreground of the employees' attention. At the time of the new manager's appointment, an international union was in the middle of a campaign to organize the plant.

One of the general manager's comments on his first days in his new job was: "When I used to walk into the office in those days no one would smile or speak to me or anyone else. No one really felt they belonged to the team here." It was an organization in which work was a grim process.[2]

The grimness of the work did not arise, it is to be noted, out of the physical condition of the plant or out of the wage scale, but from the lack of teamwork. Effective working relationships between the members of the administrative team had not been established and confusion and frustration resulted.

This lack of teamwork was manifested all the way down to the work benches. A distinct gap existed between top management and the workers in the shop, a gap which was not being spanned effectively by "the thin bridge of supervisors, foremen, and staff specialists." This gap was caused in large measure by a lack of understanding on both sides.

For a foreman this was really a grim place to work. He was caught in a vortex, buffeted by pressures from the hourly workers on the one side and by conflicting instructions, criticisms, and pressures from the supervisor and staff specialists on the other side. Such buffeting does not produce a hospitable work climate and, parenthetically, it does not yield profits.

During the Second World War a company in another industry, which had expanded rapidly to handle military orders, was notorious in the community in which it was situated as not being a good place to work. Confusion was prevalent in the administrative staff; discipline was lax; labor turnover was high; cynicism and unrest were widespread.

In the two cases just cited the newness and the rapidity of the expansion of the industries undoubtedly contributed to

[2] Ulrich, Booz, and Lawrence, *Management Behavior and Foreman Attitude*, p. 9.

the causes for the unsatisfactory work climate. But analogous situations also are to be found in some long-established industries. In one venerable cotton manufacturing company, for instance, the president who took over the top management job in the 1920's lacked the judgment and the forthrightness to retain the loyalty and support of the operating staff, and the morale of the whole enterprise gradually deteriorated. In a large company in another textile industry, for many years internal politics were rife; the managers of the various plants were seeking to cut one another's throats and the plant managers and purchasing officers often were at serious odds with the sales department and with the officers at headquarters.

In still another industry, shortly after a new president was installed, a man from outside the company, a wholesale firing of junior executives and office workers occurred. The manner in which this action was taken caused wide resentment and impaired the morale of the whole force.

Within a single company working conditions may be favorable for many of the officers and employees but unattractive to others. One large and highly prosperous corporation, for instance, some years ago hired several young men with a training for business management. Those young men properly were given elementary, routine assignments. They had to serve an apprenticeship on such work before they could qualify for wider experience and eventually for advancement. After these young men were hired apparently they were forgotten; their apprenticeships turned into seemingly long-term sentences and they became unhappy. Recently I have learned that highly trained young scientists have been going through the same sort of experiences in that company. Consequently that is not looked upon by informed persons as a good place for able young men to go to work.

Some twenty years ago a manufacturing company in the

grocery field hired several college men who were given initial assignments as missionary salesmen. Their tasks were to check the stocks of retailers and to obtain orders for promotional items to be filled through wholesalers. That too was a useful apprenticeship. After a time, however, the novelty wore off and all these men became restless. They were finding no intellectual challenge in the work. When one of them asked his district manager about future prospects, he was told that if he was patient and stuck to the job to which he was assigned for ten years or so he might have a chance to become a district manager himself.

The district manager in that instance was a man of estimable character and competent to supervise the routine selling of groceries. But he was a plodder without much vision. He had attained the height of his ambition and apparently he expected all the men working under him to be content to plod the same path.

In contrast to the foregoing experiences, another grocery manufacturing company has hired a considerable number of similarly trained men over a period of twenty years but with quite different results. This latter company likewise has started the men out on routine assignments in order for them to learn something about the business and to become accustomed to its operating methods. Then after a proper interval the men have been shifted to other assignments, until eventually each found a place on one of the lower rungs of the administrative ladder where he could apply his ability and his training to good advantage. The men were constantly being developed and their interest in the work was stimulated. Several of those men now hold key positions in the organization. For them the work climate was a stimulating one.

Numerous other examples of both depressing and stimulating work climates could be cited, but the examples that have been given should be sufficient to indicate that human relations and opportunities for development as well as physical environment and economic factors constitute important elements in the work climate.

It is difficult to apply a yardstick to morale or to measure its effects. It does influence both the quantity and quality of the work done, however, and it markedly affects labor turnover and various other items of cost. Of by no means the least significance is the relation between morale and administrative wear and tear.

Enthusiasm and loyalty

When enthusiasm for the job and loyalty to the company permeate the administrative organization, the factory crew, the office staff, and the sales force, the work climate is a favorable one. It is a function of executive leadership to foster such an attitude of enthusiasm and loyalty. While most employees in all grades fairly can be assumed to have an inherent disposition to work harmoniously together for the success of the enterprise, potentially disruptive forces also are likely to be present. Unless they are counteracted, petty jealousies, misunderstandings, personal frustrations, and various other factors can give rise to disharmony, discontent, and unrest. Under the stresses and strains of changing conditions and the exigencies of competition, furthermore, the insidious dangers of these disruptive forces only too frequently are overlooked or neglected.

One of the first requisites for a stimulating of enthusiasm and loyalty is an understanding by the executives of the point of view, the attitudes, the problems, and the reactions of the human beings who constitute the working forces of the company. In many a small enterprise the proprietor or manager knows every employee personally, and an effective basis for mutual understanding is established. The employee can ask for information and offer suggestions which he knows will be given serious consideration. The boss for his part has a real acquaintance with the points of view and the reactions of the workers. Thus he is in a position to stimulate enthusiasm and generate loyalty.

Such idyllic conditions are by no means universal among small concerns. The head of a small enterprise may be a small man, with little gift for understanding the points of view and problems of others. Acquaintanceship does not necessarily result in understanding, and the gift of understanding is far from being a universal human attribute. But if the head of a small enterprise does possess that gift of understanding, he does not have to combat remoteness in exercising it.

The head of a large corporation may or may not have the gift of understanding the points of view and the problems of the rank and file of the workers. He may have been selected because of proficiency in finance, or engineering, or some other specialty, where the emphasis is not on human relations. But even when the chief executive of a large company has an aptitude for human understanding, he necessarily is so far removed from the workers in the factory and the salesmen in the field that special arrangements have to be provided if he is to maintain a real and constant understanding of their points of view and of their attitudes. The lines of communication are long and tenuous and easily can become clogged or broken.

The executive's lieutenants, in a business of any size, therefore must become his deputies in dealing with many of these problems of human relations which so vitally affect morale. This arrangement does not relieve the chief executive of ultimate responsibility for an understanding of these problems. His deputies will give these problems the attention which they deserve only if they are instructed and coached to deal with them and to discuss with the boss critical situations when they develop. Hence it is through his lieutenants and his working relationships with the lieutenants that the executive sets the tone for the human relations of the whole outfit.

In order to ascertain whether anything in my own range of experience would shed further light on this problem of stimulating enthusiasm and loyalty, I have put down a list of twenty-four executives, chiefly in the field of business, with whom I have been associated or acquainted intimately enough to permit me to form a judgment on the enthusiasm and loyalty of their organizations. I then rated them roughly and came up with nine A's, five B's, eight C's, and two D's. My grading, of course, is not infallible, but since I do not intend to reveal in any way who was on the list, I shall not have to defend my ratings. To me it looks as though there may be a significant range of experience in this little group of examples.

First, let's take some of the C's. One of them, for instance, was a well-intentioned, broad-minded individual, who had an almost incredible number of acquaintances, many of them distinguished or influential. He had inherited his position, and with it a considerable fortune. He worked reasonably hard, but not very successfully. He typified the era when C was considered to be the gentleman's grade in college. He was a gentleman. But most of his associates in business did not take him very seriously. His good intentions could not make up for the muddiness in his mind. Need I point out the effect on enthusiasm and morale in the organization?

Quite in contrast to the preceding example was Roger, another in my C category. Roger did not have an opportunity to go to college. Instead, because of his family's meager income, he went to work in a factory when he was sixteen years old. When he was fifty, he was president of the company, a self-made man. He had acquired something of a fortune, so that from the standpoint of position and wealth he could be deemed successful. Some of his close friends have told me that he really was a very kindhearted man. But in conducting his business affairs he was a niggardly, penny-pinching slave driver. He was strictly honest, but he also was ruthless in demanding what he held to be his rights. He was cynical and tactless, and he had only limited resourcefulness for meeting changing conditions. The corporation did not prosper under his management, and so long as he was president, the morale of the organization was low.

To run over some of the others in my C group rather hurriedly, three of them, I find, were well-meaning individuals who did not have the vision and resourcefulness to enable them to master the adversities of a changing world. One of the three, I discovered after a rather prolonged acquaintanceship, also was somewhat deficient in intellectual honesty. He was reluctant to admit even to himself certain unfavorable results which could be corrected only if they were faced squarely. Such traits as that are sensed sooner or later by enough people in an organization to cause an impairment of morale. Morale is nurtured by enduring qualities of character, and any deficiency in those qualities stunts its growth.

Another executive of my acquaintance was ingenious, imaginative, genial, a hard worker, and apparently a public-spirited citizen. When I learned eventually that in his organization there was little enthusiasm and a rather marked absence of loyalty, I was quite surprised. On further observation, however, I concluded that he had carried over into his internal operations a certain tricky ingenuity which had appeared from time to time in his outside dealings. He had built up the business himself from a very small beginning and in his ambitious struggle to survive he had resorted occasionally to moves which best can be described as tricky, not technically dishonest, just tricky.

The executive of another company, a large corporation, was promoted from the treasurership to the presidency at a time when the company was going through the greatest vicissitudes that it had experienced in seventy years. As president his chief effort was directed toward conserving the company's cash. His attitude, however, was essentially a defeatist one. His office and the treasurer's office were located in Boston, the sales office in New York, and the plants in four scattered cities. Many of the most difficult problems focused around the New York office, and occasionally a proposal was made that he should move his headquarters to New York. After his return from his next weekly visit to New York, however, he would shake his head and state emphatically that he could not endure spending any more time in that madhouse. In effect, he ducked taking any real responsibility for securing teamwork between his lieutenants, and without teamwork there could be little enthusiasm and loyalty in the organization. His defeatist attitude was contagious.

My final exhibit in the C group is another self-made man, highly successful from the standpoint of accumulating wealth. He was an unusually imaginative person, honest and sincere. The morale of his organization, however, was mediocre, a condition which I attribute to several factors. In the first place, when he started the business on an experimental basis he felt that he had to hire "cheap help." He had a somewhat niggardly disposition, except when entertaining nabobs or other persons of distinction, and he continued to employ "cheap help," without offering incentives commensurate with the opportunities. In the second place, he was a somewhat unstable person. His active imagination led him frequently to start some new project long before the last one had been completed, a habit disconcerting to the organization. This executive, finally, was an unusually shrewd judge of the probable reactions of masses of people, but typically he did not have a sympathetic understanding of the point of view of a particular individual. It is of such apparent paradoxes, of course, that "human nature" is made up, and those consoling inconsistencies in others help to make life endurable for the rest of us imperfect mortals. For the subject in hand, this exhibit serves to remind us that rewards commensurate with achievement, executive stability, and a sympathetic comprehension of the point of view of key individuals also are among the factors which help to generate enthusiasm and loyalty.

One of the executives whom I placed in the D category on morale rating also inherited his position. He was a forceful individual, with a strong presence and, apparently, an abundance of self-confidence. In his early years as an executive he was rated as one of the leaders in his industry, but eventually it developed that his management was not so good as his speeches and that his company was slipping. When the company struck rough going, particularly in the early 1930's, an impaired morale was revealed. This executive glibly presented alibis which at first appeared plausible, but which later palled. Eventually I observed streaks of yellow in some of his dealings.

My other executive in the D category, I regret to admit, was a college president, a man whom I never met personally but with some of whose staff I was intimately acquainted. This gentleman not only was lacking in executive competency on several counts, but he was somewhat two-faced, a characteristic which does not engender loyalty and enthusiasm.

In the organizations which I rated B in enthusiasm and loyalty, there was evidence of a moderate amount of enthusiasm and no disloyalty. The morale was good but not excellent. The executives of the several organizations in this group as well as the executives of the organizations in the other groups shared in the responsibility for the state of morale in their respective concerns.

The president of one of the B enterprises was an able, vigorous promoter, and under his management the company had grown to be one of the largest in the industry. Unfortunately, however, he could not resist the temptation to intrude frequently into the precincts of his lieutenants and to meddle with the performance of tasks assigned to them. Those intrusions dampened the enthusiasm of several of the lieutenants and the attitude of the lieutenants was reflected down the line.

The presidents of two other corporations in this group, both very able men, seemed to lack that touch of human understanding which could have sparked real enthusiasm.

Among the executives of the companies in the A group there were, of course, substantial variations in personalities, in aptitudes, and in methods. In their leadership typically they avoided the weaknesses revealed in the situations already summarized, and they showed conspicuously such qualities as sincerity, fair-mindedness, courage to face facts, resourcefulness, and vision.

Sincerity and fair-mindedness are essential for the inspiring of confidence, without which there can be little enthusiasm. If we had not been so bedeviled politically for twenty years by various "Deals," I should use the term "square deal" here, because confidence among the lieutenants that each will receive a square deal is one of the bases for enthusiasm and loyalty. If there is confidence among the lieutenants that each will be treated squarely, with no favoritism, a spirit is generated which may permeate the entire organization. This sort of square treatment involves settling disputes or conflicts on their merits and also giving opportunities to those who deserve them.

Several years ago I had occasion to interview all the senior executives and numerous junior executives of a highly prosperous company with sales of more than fifty million dollars a year. Without exception every one of those interviewed referred to the president as "a wonderful man." They demonstrated a high personal regard for his integrity, his judgment, his foresight, and his fairness. He was a hard driver, to be sure, but they were his loyal, devoted supporters. With him, they always knew where they stood, and that was an incentive to give their best. They felt certain that they would be treated squarely.

Although most of us are disposed to grumble a bit when we have to work hard, nevertheless hard work is conducive to a growth of loyalty and enthusiasm, provided there is confidence in the fairness of the administration and in the attainment of worth-while results. Recently I had an opportunity to chat with a professor at a college where a new president had been installed a couple of years before. I had known the president well before he took on his new job, so naturally I was interested in learning how he was making out with his faculty. In reply to my question, the professor stated that the president was a man of integrity, ideas, and ideals, with a drive to get results. For me that is a terse recipe for loyalty and enthusiasm.

The spark of achievement

An official of one of the major league baseball clubs, currently rather low in the standings, is reported to have said: "We have some good ball players here, but too many of them are nice fellows with no spirit." Nice fellows with no spirit do not win many ball games, and nice fellows with no spirit also do not achieve many victories in the turmoil of business competition.

In business there is a need for a will to win on the part of both the executive and his lieutenants. If both have that will, they can infuse it into the rest of the organization and into the rank and file of the employees. If both the executive and his lieutenants do not have that will to win, there is no likelihood that that spirit will appear significantly anywhere in the enterprise.

In the case of one company which had been experiencing losses, the president was dismissed and one of the senior officers promoted to the presidency. The directors apparently were especially impressed with his honesty and integrity. The losses which the company had encountered, however, had in fact broken his spirit. Essentially he had become a defeatist. In the organization was a group of younger men who had considerable resourcefulness and in whom a will to win readily could have been kindled. Eventually most of them became discouraged by the defeatist attitude of the president and left for positions in more stimulating climates.

In the case of another company, which also had suffered from low earnings, the retirement of the president was forced by a state of poor health. None of the other executives appeared to be qualified to fill the vacancy, and a man was brought in from outside. He was imbued with a spirit of success, and when he became convinced that several of the department heads did not likewise have a will to win, "the nice fellows with no spirit" were replaced. After that change was made the group became a much harder hitting team with a real spark of achievement.

In certain large corporations the spark of achievement has become so traditional that "nice fellows with no spirit" are sidetracked early. The stimulus arising out of that tradition and the process of executive selection which it engenders constitute real advantages for those corporations. When all the members of the team are imbued with a confidence that they can and will win and have a tradition of making good on that confidence, they have a real edge on other contenders.

Not all large corporations have such a traditional spirit of achievement. One of the largest corporations in the United States, for example, which attained its eminence by merger rather than by growth, for several decades had no such tradition and frequently lost ground to smaller competitors with keener executives. The company often was subjected to political attack, but never at its most vulnerable spot — administrative stodginess. Recently there have been several manifestations that the company has begun to develop a morale based on achievement instead of continuing to rely on mere bulk. The organization is so large, with its old point of view so deeply imbedded, that a transmutation of its morale, if it can be accomplished, will be something of a twentieth-century miracle. It will be a demonstration of executive leadership of an unusually high order.

The purpose of the foregoing reference to "big business" is merely to call attention to an especially significant aspect of some large corporations which usually is overlooked in public discussions of their affairs. Other corporations now much smaller undoubtedly will reach the "big" class eventually, partly because of the spark of achievement in their executive teams. But whether a company be large or small, an executive team of competent men sparked by a will to win will gain ground on less spirited rivals.

The mettle of an organization is constantly being tested not only by the competitive struggle but also by the challenge of changing conditions. As has been pointed out earlier, in this ever changing world survival is possible only when a business enterprise can adapt itself to its unstable environment. These environmental changes cause untold hardship, but at the same time they offer a challenging opportunity to those who have a zest for adventure and a will to win. A company where the executive organization is imbued with a zest of adventure and a will to win is likely to be a good place to work.

X

Extracurricular Activities

The main job of an executive is to administer effectively the affairs of the enterprise of which he is in charge. Nevertheless, typically he has to face many demands on his time and energy for participation in activities outside his own organization. The more successful he is in handling his primary job, the greater will be the demands on him from the outside world.

The range of extracurricular activities of business executives is so wide and so varied that an attempt will be made here to present only a few suggestive samples and to point out some of their implications. The sorts of activities to which reference is made, furthermore, include only those which are related, directly or indirectly, to business management. Those which are strictly recreational or personal are not included.

Directorates

One of the extracurricular opportunities open to many successful executives is membership on the boards of directors of other corporations. There are some corporations, to be sure, where the boards include only "insiders," that is, operating officers of the respective companies. In such instances the problem of accepting membership on other boards is not likely to arise. If a company does not include any "outsiders" on its board, it hardly would be consistent for its officers to serve on the boards of other corporations. There are numerous companies, however, in which "outsiders" are invited to accept nomination for membership on the boards,[1] and among the "outsiders" often sought as prospective directors are the executives of successful corporations which also have "outsiders" on their boards.

When an executive receives a "bid" to join the board of directors of another corporation, should he accept or decline? Is he to engage in any such extracurricular activities? If so, which "bids" should be accepted? On how many boards should he accept membership? These are some of the questions to which he will have to find answers.

An executive may well hesitate to take on any outside directorships. For one thing, a directorship involves legal liabilities which are by no means negligible. Then, too, if the responsibilities of a director are to be conscientiously performed, he must familiarize himself with the affairs of the corporation and study its financial statements and other reports so as to prepare himself to take part intelligently in the deliberations of the board. That procedure uses up time and energy which may well be needed for the performance of his regular executive duties.

In view of the burdens which a directorship places upon the conscientious incumbent, why do executives take on directorships in other companies? The financial reward is negligible, so the reasons must be sought elsewhere.

Probably the major ground on which acceptance of an outside directorship is justified in many instances is its educa-

[1] For more comprehensive discussions of directors, see John C. Baker, *Directors and Their Functions* (1945), Melvin T. Copeland and Andrew R. Towl, *The Board of Directors and Business Management* (1947), and Myles L. Mace, *The Board of Directors in Small Corporations* (1948), publications of the Division of Research, Harvard Business School, Boston.

tional value. The intimate discussions, formal and informal, of the problems of a company among the members of its board of directors with a wide variety of backgrounds and experiences can have a stimulating and broadening effect on an alert member of the board. An executive of another company who is a member of the board not only can contribute his views to the discussion but he can pick up ideas and concepts which will help him on his own administrative job. The normal intellectual give and take of such discussions has a real potential educational value.

An executive, moreover, by serving on the board of directors of another corporation, may learn to see more clearly his own position in relation to the directors of his own company. By serving in a reversed position, he may observe how his own administrative techniques can be improved.

Another advantage often to be gained from acceptance of an outside directorship is the widening of an executive's acquaintanceship. There are many situations in business administration, as well as elsewhere, in which wide acquaintance with other men of affairs is a valuable although intangible asset.

By no means the least significant of the reasons for acceptance of an outside directorship is the personal gratification which derives therefrom. There is a personal satisfaction in having an opportunity to contribute to the success of another enterprise, a satisfaction in being of service. Then, too, there is a gratifying challenge in the opportunity offered by such board membership for measuring one's powers against those of the other members. And, finally, there is the gratification which comes from being deemed worthy of such recognition, from being admitted to the club, as it were. Membership in a board of directors, in other words, often is assumed to be a token of proficiency.

If the powers that be in a corporation desire to have outside men on its board of directors — and there are good reasons in many cases for doing so — then it is only fitting that the executives of that corporation should be permitted to accept invitations to serve on the boards of some other companies when such invitations are tendered them.

Among the reasons for accepting an outside directorship, I have not included as valid one which still has influence in some quarters. I refer to reciprocal dealing arrangements, business-getting objectives, and favor-currying hopes. The function of a board of directors broadly is to direct the management of the affairs of the corporation. If a person accepts election to membership on a board of directors of a corporation with any purpose in view other than that of providing the best management possible for that corporation, he is not accepting his responsibilities in good faith. A company, furthermore, which has to resort to such devices to effect sales or to achieve some surreptitious objective is not likely to be a company where an outside executive can enhance his reputation or strengthen his managerial power by membership on the board.

On how many outside boards can an executive properly accept membership? This is a question which causes perplexity and embarrassment to some executives who are much sought after as directors. Obviously an executive cannot devote all his time to this extracurricular activity. But where is he to draw the line? And how can he draw a line without causing offense or hurting the feelings of those who issue the invitations. It is a delicate task to accept some "bids" and to turn down others.

In determining where to draw the line in accepting "bids" an executive has three sets of interests to weigh. First, his duties as an executive. Will acceptance of an additional directorship interfere with the fulfillment of his executive responsibilities? That is the primary consideration. Second, the duties of a director. Will he be able and willing to devote enough time and effort to assure his giving proper attention to the affairs of the corporation for which he is invited to serve as a director? This is a matter of good faith. Third, his own personal welfare. Will the experience to be gained and the service to be rendered fully offset the wear and tear of such an additional load?

In the course of the research on directors and their problems in which I participated, no instance came to my attention in which an executive had neglected his executive duties in order to serve as a director of other corporations. There well may be such cases, but they have not come to my attention. On the other hand, I did encounter several instances in which an executive apparently had lightheartedly taken on more directorships than he was competent to handle.

One young executive, for example, an able man who had risen fast, seemed to have taken on several directorships without realization of the amount of "homework" which should have been put in in preparation for board meetings. Like many another director he was relying on his spot judgment for fulfilling his duties as a director. Of course some spot judgments have to be made by directors as unforeseen problems arise. But a director who makes only spot judgments, without previous study and analysis of the problems, is not likely to raise many searching questions or to make many truly constructive proposals. Overreliance on spot judgments reflects a rather dangerous inflation of the ego.

A few months after the publication of *The Board of Directors and Business Management,* in the writing of which I had participated, I was informed that one executive who was an outside director of several corporations had remarked that if he tried to perform the duties of a director as set forth in that report, he would have no time left for his regular job. I was not surprised that that executive was annoyed and perhaps peeved by the conclusions reached in that study. He was prone to rely on spot judgments, and it was to be expected that anything which questioned his habits and disturbed his strong self-confidence would be rather unwelcome to him. His remark was a tacit admission that he had overindulged in this type of extracurricular acitivity.

The subject of the managerial responsibilities of directors, as distinct from their legal responsibilities, is a subject to which far too little attention has been given until recently even by directors themselves. A noticeable change now is taking place, however, and numerous directors are looking at those responsibilities in a new light, and some of the executives who hold outside directorships undoubtedly will revise their views regarding this extracurricular activity. One result of this reconsideration may well be to reduce the number of outside directorships which some of these executives now hold. Perhaps it also will follow that a considerable number of boards will undergo a reduction in size, an outcome of potential merit.

Business associations

Trade associations, chambers of commerce, local, state, and national industrial organizations, and other types of business associations provide opportunities for extracurricular activities for business executives, and acceptance of some of those opportunities commonly is inescapable. By some of those ironical twists to which my fate always seems to have been subjected, it happens that I have had a rather extensive experience with these business associations, and I have been virtually forced to observe some thousands of executives participating in these activities.

Although I am not a talented public speaker, I have been called upon to make addresses before several hundred of these organizations over a period of thirty-five years. These addresses have grown out of the research work on which I have been engaged or out of certain public activities with which I have been concerned. Although I am not naturally a "joiner," I have had occasion to mix extensively with those who thrive on the promotion of membership campaigns.

While attending these meetings I have listened to probably ten times as many speeches as I have made myself. I have sat through many business meetings, and in the hotel and convention hall lobbies I have listened to innumerable informal discussions. There I have seen and heard business executives of many types, big and little, liberal and tory, foresighted and hindsighted. Some thirty years ago I even was offered a job as secretary of a national trade association, and to his dying day the chairman of the committee which made me the offer could not comprehend why I turned down a job that would have paid me a salary twice what I was then receiving at the university. As for the banquets, so called, I shudder at the mere thought of fried chicken and Delmonico potatoes. All these experiences have given me at least some acquaintance with this type of extracurricular activity of business executives and some familiarity with the atmosphere in which those activities are carried on.

Many association meetings are drab and dull, but occasionally eruptions occur which suffice to make the meetings interesting. Unwittingly I myself sometimes have been the cause of such an eruption. One such experience occurred in St. Louis about twenty-five years ago, at a meeting of the Controllers' Congress — an organization of department store controllers. The subject of my talk, suggested by the program chairman, was: "Is it true that the cost of doing business is higher in the large stores?" That subject had been proposed because of the early results of our study of operating expenses of department stores which showed the ratio of expense to sales to be higher in the big stores. I gave my address, presenting my statistical evidence and giving my interpretation of the reasons for such a result.

The chairman of that meeting, who was controller of one of the largest department stores in New York City, hardly could wait for me to finish my talk so that he could turn the chair over to another controller and take the platform to answer me. He proclaimed emphatically how wrong I was. Such a result just could not be true, he said. And he added that if my conclusions were valid, he would not dare to return to New York. Subsequently, at dinner I had an opportunity to tell him and the other controllers in a friendly spirit that I bore him no ill will but that he might as well stay in St. Louis. He did go back to New York, but twenty-five years later, just as he was retiring from his controllership, he sent word to me by a mutual friend that he had come to the conclusion that the statements which I had made in St. Louis back in 1924 really were correct. Age had tempered his emotions.

In looking over the whole field there may seem to be a plethora of business associations, with extensive overlapping of functions. Freedom in forming associations and clubs, however, is part of our American birthright, a privilege which is exercised freely by college professors, the womenfolk, and other groups as well as businessmen. Some of these associations are organized and maintained, I have learned, primarily to provide jobs for the secretaries and glory for the officers, but after all those organizations are rather harmless amusements.

In many associations the large companies in the respective industries are relatively inactive and their executives seldom serve as officers. They cannot afford the time consumed by the petty politics of many an association. One of the observations, furthermore, which was particularly impressed on me early in my experience with trade associations, was the number of instances in which the executives who were most actively engaged in this sort of extracurricular work were not especially successful in operating their own businesses. That statement is by no means universally true, of course, for there are numerous able executives who devote a good deal of time and energy to association work, and in times of emergency they generally come to the fore. Nevertheless, it is a fact, according to my observations, that association activities do serve as an emotional outlet for certain types of executives who suffer from feelings of frustration or inferiority.

The number of association offices and committee memberships which a business executive holds is no clue to his competency. As former Governor Saltonstall remarked to me when we were discussing possible selections for a certain position during the Second World War, a multiplicity of association positions and committee memberships may merely indicate that a man "is spreading his butter pretty thin."

My purpose in referring to the personal motivations which induce some business executives to utilize association activities as escape valves is not to imply any criticism of those motivations, but merely to call attention to the human complexities of these extracurricular activities.

On the constructive side, the services of business associations are typically educational in character. First, these associations serve as a means of educating their members on new developments of common interest, on problems of common concern, and on opportunities for improving their managerial methods. Almost every daily newspaper carries announcements and reports regarding meetings of business associations. And various other journals refer to them at least occasionally. Those announcements and reports indicate the scope and variety of the topics presented at such meetings. The informal discussions, furthermore, which take place between members at lunch and dinner and elsewhere outside the convention hall provide by no means the least effective opportunities for mutual education.

These associations also frequently undertake to inform the public regarding the problems and the points of view of the members. The effectiveness with which this particular service is performed varies greatly between associations. Some groups indulge in such crude special pleading and present their cases in such a narrow and bigoted manner that they antagonize more people than they convince of the soundness of their cause. They even make life harder for those associations which are seeking to present their cases in a fair, broad, and unexaggerated manner. Here is a field in which executive leadership of a high order has an opportunity for effecting great improvements. The obstacles to be overcome in bringing about these improvements, however, are by no means slight. For one thing, the internal politics of many an association tend to bring its public educational work down to mediocrity. In order to maintain the support and collect the dues of all the members, the educational program may have to be beamed rather low. In fact educational steps often are needed within the membership before a broad-gauge public educational program is launched. But admission of that fact only emphasizes the old dilemma. Those who need education most are likely to be the ones who appreciate it least. As has been indicated, these associations provide an extraordinarily faithful mirror of human nature in the gross.

The third type of educational work performed by business associations involves furnishing information to legislative bodies regarding measures of interest to members of the association. The breadth of view taken and the constructiveness of the attitude manifested in the presentation of such information reflect the quality of the executive leadership in the industry or in the business community represented in the association.

Representation in many association activities is delegated, of course, to their lieutenants by the top executives in all but the smaller corporations. Nevertheless there are numerous situations in which it is not easy or perhaps expedient for the top executive to delegate representation to a lieutenant. This residue can accumulate into a heavy load. When representation is delegated to a lieutenant, furthermore, the chief executive does not necessarily relieve himself of the whole burden. He still may have to confer with his lieutenant regarding the positions to be taken on various matters which are to come before the association. And, he may have to attend the annual convention at least for social reasons.

In the case of one large wholesalers' association, for instance, not only the heads of the wholesale firms but also the top executives of the leading manufacturing companies which have their products distributed through these wholesale firms regularly attend the annual convention banquet. It is quite a social affair and participation in it has substantial business significance. In numerous other business associations there are no such social appendages, but where they do occur they cannot lightly be neglected by high-ranking executives.

In drawing the line beyond which not to go in association activities, some of the shrewder executives whom I have observed seem to have set up for themselves, perhaps more or less unconsciously, such rules as the following:

(1) To accept no association assignment merely to gratify the executive's personal pride or to put him in the limelight.

(2) To accept no assignment which merely affords an opportunity to talk, with little likelihood of constructive action.

(3) To accept no assignment which serves primarily to provide an alibi for side-stepping or delaying difficult or unpleasant tasks called for by the executive's primary job.

(4) To accept no assignment merely to oblige a friend. There are limits beyond which the claims of friendship properly do not extend.

(5) To accept no nominal assignment which amounts in substance to lending his name to a project in the conduct of which he will take no active part. He realizes that, like a woman's virtue, a name that is lent freely presently loses its luster.

(6) He realizes also that an executive who "spreads his butter thin" in extracurricular activities lessens confidence in himself and in his company among the more substantial members of the community.

(7) He asks himself, when considering a proposed assignment, whether acceptance of the assignment will enable him to handle his regular job better, by broadening his perspective, by yielding new, worth-while acquaintances, by an exchange of experiences, or by other means.

(8) He asks himself whether acceptance will substantially enhance the good will of the company.

(9) He asks how acceptance of the assignment will promote the interests of the company of which he is an executive.

(10) He asks himself whether the project is one which will be of real service to the community.

Association activities offer many opportunities for constructive service by business executives. The wisdom which an executive exercises in his choice of opportunities for association activity is one manifestation of the quality of his leadership ability.

Civic and philanthropic activities

This area includes such activities as part-time service on committees and boards set up by local, state, and federal governments and active participation in the work of such agencies as community funds, hospitals, the Red Cross, and many other civic enterprises. Nowadays business executives are expected to provide a substantial share of the manpower for directing such activities, and much of this labor must be performed during normal working hours; it cannot all, or even largely, be relegated to night work. The demands on business executives for service of this sort are both a tribute to their managerial reputations and an evidence of the dependence of the community on business corporations.

Here again I have had some opportunity to observe business executives in action, particularly on government committees and boards. Perhaps a few of these experiences may be worth citing.

One of the first of these experiences was as a member of the Massachusetts Commission on the Cost of Living appointed by Governor McCall in the autumn of 1916. That was a small commission of five members. Two of the members were businessmen who were by no means novices in the political field; two were interested primarily in politics, although they also had other professional occupations; and I was a green young assistant professor, with no political experience and no political aspirations. My appointment was made, I understood, on the recommendation of Dean Gay, who apparently relished thrusting me into new experiences whatever the risk might be. Apparently I was expendable.

I learned several things from service on that commission, in addition to certain facts regarding prices. For example, I made a proposal to the other members one day for a recommendation for a new organization to be set up to prepare for the growing threat of war emergency. My proposal was rejected summarily at the instance of the leading businessman on the commission. Three days later the establishment of an organization such as I had proposed was announced by the Governor with that businessman as its chairman. I had not made my initial proposal through the right channels, but I was learning.

I also learned how careful one with political ambitions has to be in his informal associations. One member of the commission, for example, did not care to be seen lunching with a certain other member of the commission.

Toward the end of the brief existence of that commission, I had a telephone call from a reporter on the most sensational newspaper in Boston asking me what information we had regarding a man whom I will call Mr. Doakes. I have not the slightest recollection now of what his real name was. In my innocence I asked the reporter who Mr. Doakes was. I had never heard of him. Thereupon there was a snort from the reporter and a termination of the conversation. The next edition of his paper carried a large headline announcing that a member of the Commission on the Cost of Living had never heard of Mr. Doakes, the man who "scratched the back of every hog" coming into the state and who therefore allegedly was responsible for the high price of pork. I was beginning to be initiated into the ways of reporters.

During the next two years I was in Washington, first as secretary of the Commercial Economy Board of the Council of National Defense, later as executive secretary of the Conservation Division of the War Industries Board. There I learned more about reporters. One businessman, for example, who was almost literally killing himself in facilitating the procurement of supplies for the armed forces as a member of the staff of the War Industries Board, was too busy and too impatient to find time for interviews with reporters. That made some of the reporters angry, and they vowed vengeance. Later, when Congressional hearings were held at which that businessman was called upon to testify, some of the newspaper reports played up the occasional mistakes which he had made and said nothing about his really substantial achievement. He was virtually crucified because he had not availed himself at the proper time of the opportunities to acquaint the news reporters with his work.

When a business executive engages in this type of extracurricular activity he learns that it is not enough to perform his assignment competently; he must also learn how to deal with the press.

Then, too, if he is in Washington, he must learn how to deal with congressmen. Most of the work of our Conservation Division, which continued and expanded the program started under the Council of National Defense, was not sufficiently spectacular to attract much attention from congressmen. My tightest squeeze there occurred on a very hot forenoon in the summer of 1918. Mr. Shaw, the chairman of the Division, was away from the city so that I was in charge. About eleven o'clock I received word from the reception desk that Congressman Sabath was there with several of his constituents, so I met with them, of course. I had a high regard for the Congressman, and I knew that he was taking a friendly interest in the activities of the Division.

The constituents whom he introduced were retailers from the lower west side in Chicago. The spokesman proceeded to recommend that we issue an order banning the use of trading stamps, and he set forth the alleged advantages which would accrue from such action. I had no particular interest in trading stamps, and I could not see how the discontinuance of their use would substantially promote the war effort. A flat announcement to that effect, however, seemed to me to be inexpedient. Consequently, by asking an occasional question, I was able to keep the conference going while I was searching for a solution. Finally, I explained that our Division had no mandatory power. All our programs were put into effect by voluntary coöperation. That point, parenthetically, was particularly important at that moment, because numerous bitter complaints recently had been voiced in Congress against agencies which were exceeding their legal powers.

I then asked the spokesman whether it would be possible to effect a discontinuance of trading stamps by voluntary action of the retailers themselves, since we had no mandatory power. The spokesman enthusiastically replied that such a discontinuance could be effected voluntarily, but I noticed that two of his party were shaking their heads. The delegation then entered upon a spirited argument among themselves regarding the possibility of voluntary discontinuance. The others finally convinced the spokesman that it could not be done voluntarily. Whereupon all I had to do was to point out to the Congressman that since a mandatory order seemed necessary, Congressional action would be needed; it was beyond our power. Whereupon the Congressman smiled benignly, and he and his constituents left with no hard feelings.

I have found that members of Congress generally are very fair in their attitudes regarding the treatment of their constituents by government officials, provided the constituents are given fair hearings and courteous consideration.

Membership on one of these government commissions, furthermore, sometimes presents perplexing problems of dealing with other businessmen, some of whom have a complexity of motivations. When an emissary from Governor Saltonstall first conferred with me in the fall of 1941 regarding the organization of the Committee on Postwar Readjustment, it was contemplated that the commission would have a membership of about twelve. In order to provide representation, however, for a variety of industrial, labor, and educational groups, government departments, and other interests, we wound up with an initial membership of thirty-three. As soon as the appointments were announced, several other gentlemen volunteered their services as members of the committee, but no additions were made. Had the door been reopened, I suspect that the volunteers would have swamped us. All these volunteers wished to make a patriotic contribution of their time and effort, but some of them also were motivated by a liking for the limelight.

The applications of most of the volunteers presented no serious problem. One business executive from a city outside of Boston, however, was persistent. After his initial offer of service had been declined, he enlisted the support of another businessman whose unofficial political activities had given him great influence on Beacon Hill. At the request of that influential personage, I held an interview with the applicant but was able to placate him without adding to the size of the committee.

In 1948 I ran into another problem of membership volunteers. In July of that year I was asked informally whether I would be willing to serve on an advisory council which the Trade Policies Subcommittee of the Senate Interstate and Foreign Commerce Committee was planning to organize. Senator Capehart was chairman of the Senate subcommittee, the task of which was to examine the need for clarification of the law regarding the use of delivered prices and freight absorption which seemingly had been thrown into confusion by the dicta of the Supreme Court in the Cement Case.

Since that subject was one to which I had given a good deal of attention for nearly thirty years, I indicated a willingness to serve on such an advisory council, which was to have twelve to fifteen members, I understood. A few days later I received a telephone call, asking me to serve as chairman of the advisory council: I accepted and two weeks later went to Washington to meet with the Senators and to make plans for scheduling the first meeting. There it appeared that the size of the advisory council was to be increased, first to twenty-five members, then to thirty-five as a maximum. Ten days later, the membership was announced — forty-two; and that subsequently was raised to forty-six.

Such a large group was unwieldy, of course, particularly since its membership included a number of prima donnas. The large size did have one great advantage, however. Since most of the members were substantially respected in their communities and their industries, the large membership served to acquaint a great many businessmen and labor leaders with the seriousness of the disruption with which many industries would be faced if the theories of certain members of the staff of the Federal Trade Commission, as accepted in the dicta of the Supreme Court, were to become imbedded in the law. The advisory council served an educational purpose quite different but perhaps even more valuable than the one that was originally intended.

These committees and commissions often may seem to be time-consuming and cumbersome, and I certainly would not defend them as examples of streamlined efficiency or as soporific remedies for a light-sleeping chairman. Nevertheless, they are the antithesis of dictatorship. They have both the defects and the merits of their democratic processes. They at least afford opportunities for presentation of diverse points of view and for discussion of wide scope on problems of public concern. They constitute one form of democratic representation.

The groups to which I have referred constitute only a tiny sample, of course, of all civic activities in which business executives are called upon to participate. And my experiences very likely may not have been typical. But even if they were not typical they at least illustrate some of the diversities of such activities and indicate the sort of atmosphere in which those activities take place.

The circumstances surrounding the formation of each such

group, the auspices under which it is organized, the apparent opportunity for worth-while achievement, and the freedom for independent action, all are considerations which are taken into account by a levelheaded business executive in deciding whether to accept nomination for membership. In some situations the issue at stake is of such transcendent significance that an executive actually has little choice in deciding whether to serve. In the bulk of the cases, however, he can weigh the reasons for serving against the other demands on his limited time and energy.

Organized philanthropies constitute still another category of activities in which business executives, especially successful business executives, are expected to take a prominent part. Most business executives desire to be of service to their communities and therefore participate in the work of local philanthropic organizations. But any one executive seldom can accept all the opportunities for such service offered to him. As is the case with other extracurricular activities, he must pick and choose those where he can make the maximum contribution with a minimum interference with his primary task, which is to administer successfully the affairs of the business of which he is in charge. Unless he continues to be a successful executive, he will not long be in real demand for active participation in civic and philanthropic activities. The examples of service rendered by business executives in philanthropic organizations are so numerous, however, that mere reference to them suffices for a reminder of the part that they play in the lives of those executives.

All these extracurricular activities, such as membership on boards of directors and service with business associations and with civic and philanthropic groups, constitute an integral part of the job of most business executives. Recognition of these activities emphasizes the fact that a business concern is a social enterprise, with far-reaching ramifications. Its activities are interwoven in a broad social fabric, where the opportunities for constructive service by executive leaders are legion.

XI

Standards of Conduct

The administrative load which he carries plus the demands on his time and energy for participation in extracurricular activities places a severe strain on both the physical and moral stamina of many a business executive. His moral stamina is particularly tested by the exigencies of keeping the wheels turning in an ever changing environment, where competition frequently takes new and unexpected turns, and where so many vagaries of human nature are encountered both within the organization and without. Amid these unrelenting pressures, temptation ever is whispering suggestions that a corner be cut here, that a sharp practice be indulged in there, or that some shady deal be countenanced yon. Ability to withstand such temptations is one of the major requisites for executive achievement.

Confidence and integrity

The organization of a modern business enterprise is predicated upon confidence in the integrity and good faith of its executives, from the top all the way down through the successive ranks. Although a system of control checks is set up, such a system works successfully only when there is merely an occasional malefactor to be caught. A control system, in fact, serves primarily to reveal errors and misunderstandings and to furnish guiding information rather than to detect unfaithfulness and dishonesty.

The very term "organization" connotes mutual confidence between the executive leader and his lieutenants and between the lieutenants and their subordinates. Unless an executive can trust a lieutenant to carry out instructions and policies in good faith, to the best of his understanding and ability, the lieutenant is a liability rather than an aid. Similarly, unless a lieutenant can rely upon his superior officer to fulfill his obligations and commitments, the lieutenant and his associates can only flounder in a rough sea of uncertainty. Without a dependable leader no one can count with assurance on anyone else to perform his tasks in good faith. In the absence of leadership, there can only be chaos, the very antithesis of "organization." Moreover, unless moral integrity and a spirit of fair play engendered by the leader predominate over narrow selfish considerations in the management of an enterprise, mutual confidence and the group spirit which is so essential to success will not be present.

In the scandalous case of McKesson & Robbins, Inc., in the 1930's, the depredations of Mr. Coster-Musica while president failed to wreck the enterprise only because the other executives, with a couple of exceptions, and the heads of the operating units were men of proved integrity. These other executives had established their reputations before their firms were lured into the merger. After the scandal broke they were absolved of all blame. They too had been victimized by a clever and dishonest manipulator. But their reputations were unsmirched, so they could take over the responsibility for managing the company and rehabilitating its reputation.

The standards of conduct of an executive beget like standards for his subordinates. An executive with upright standards of conduct attracts other upright men to work with him, and he inspires them to strengthen their uprightness.

Executives such as John Wanamaker, Marshall Field, Owen D. Young, George Eastman, and George F. Baker, to name only a few of the long list of American business leaders of high integrity, are conspicuous examples of men who inspired uprightness among their associates.

The extent to which an executive's standard of conduct may ramify through an organization is illustrated by a statement recently made by an officer of one of the largest corporations in the United States, and one particularly distinguished for upright management. He stated that as men down the line encounter new problems they are continually asking themselves such questions as the following: "What would Mr. B (the president of the company) do in this situation?" "What would be his attitude toward this proposal?" Even though many of those men never talk with Mr. B personally, they are seeking devotedly to act in accordance with his standards.

I have known Mr. B rather well for forty years. In his make-up he has nothing of a dictator or martinet. He has exercised his leadership in a quiet and unobtrusive manner. At the same time, as the attitude reflected in the foregoing statements indicates, he has inspired real loyalty in the organization. Furthermore, he always has been consistent. That consistency is significant, because it has helped to induce stability in a large group. If Mr. B ever were to step out of character and to act inconsistently with his long-established standard of conduct, the organization would soon be floundering.

In the continual process of selection of administrative personnel whereby a sound business organization is developed and maintained, the choice of candidates for appointment is governed not only by technical competency but even more by moral qualifications. Because of the nature of my own work for many years, I frequently have been called upon to answer questions regarding the qualifications of young men for junior administrative positions. In those inquiries stress invariably is placed on the honesty, integrity, and uprightness of the candidate. The reason for such stress being placed on those qualities is not primarily to guard against theft and peculation but rather to make sure that the candidate will be a faithful and dependable member of the organization.

After a man has started up the administrative ladder, furthermore, promotion is governed at least as much by reliability as by technical competency. Because of this continual sifting process, it is rare that a man attains a high executive position in a well-established company who does not measure up to a high standard of conduct.

Dependability, of course, is not merely a matter of moral stamina; in some cases it is a matter of emotional stability. A person may be thoroughly honest and sincere and also very erratic. Unfortunately some men with brilliant minds are so unstable emotionally that they cannot safely be given serious administrative responsibilities. Examples of this type are rather numerous. One man, for instance, whom I knew well thirty years ago, had a pleasant personality and a good mind, but he was somewhat unstable emotionally. His instability was aggravated by wounds suffered in the First World War. He was a most likable chap, but emotionally he could not stand the strain of administrative responsibility, and eventually he became an alcoholic.

Another man of about the same age as the one just referred to had one of the most gracious personalities that I have known. He started out as a salesman and eventually reached a position of considerable executive responsibility. His executive position opened up social opportunities for him, however, which went to his head. He then revealed an emotional instability which ruined his usefulness as an executive, and he fell much faster than he had risen.

Still another example is that of a young man who had a keen mind — so keen, in fact, that he became intellectually arrogant. He also was insufferably selfish. As a result he disqualified himself for administrative opportunities which would readily have been open to him if he could have conducted himself decently as a member of a team. His intellectual power could not make up for shallowness in character.

Emotional stability is particularly essential in a period of great stress and strain, such as in a business crisis or at a time when drastic changes in the business environment are encountered. Then a calm head and a steady hand are called for. If the boss is emotionally calm in such a period, the crew is much less likely to become panicky. Inasmuch as those periods of stress and strain often come unexpectedly, it is good insurance for a company to have a steady executive in charge at all times.

In the preceding paragraphs emphasis has been placed on confidence and integrity from the organizational point of view. Confidence also is essential to the securing of capital for most business corporations, and the granting of credit also is conditioned upon confidence and trust.

Manufacturers, wholesalers, and retailers make credit sales every year running into billions of dollars where reliance for payment rests primarily on the good faith of the buyers. Of course there are some losses from bad debts, not always indicative of bad faith, and some debts are collected through action in the courts. The great bulk of the indebtedness created by these credit sales, however, is paid faithfully by the buyers. These credit sales and their faithful payment are so commonplace that we may be prone to forget how great a part confidence plays in our daily lives. In a world torn by political dissension and distrust, it is significant, it seems to me, that so vast a volume of business is transacted on the basis of confidence and trust.

In the banking business, likewise, a substantial volume of "character loans" are made regularly. Such loans are backed primarily by the integrity of the borrowers rather than by tangible assets. In other words the security for such loans is the reputation of the borrowers for dependable standards of conduct.

Capital for many corporations is provided by investors who have faith in the competency and the integrity of the directors and the executives to whose stewardship the funds are entrusted. The American Telephone and Telegraph Company at the end of 1949 had 829,500 stockholders; Standard Oil Company (New Jersey), 215,000 stockholders; General Electric Company, 250,562 stockholders; General Motors Corporation, 434,075 stockholders; Swift & Company, 64,300 stockholders; Eastman Kodak Company, 54,234 stockholders; and Union Carbide and Carbon Corporation, 92,329 stockholders; to name only a few examples of corporations whose capital stock is widely owned. The major security of these investors is the competency and the integrity of the managers of these enterprises.

This display of confidence belies the pronouncement made by Adam Smith one hundred and seventy-five years ago. He said:

> The only trades which it seems possible for a joint stock company to carry on successfully, without an exclusive privilege, are those of which all the operations are capable of being reduced to what is called a routine, or to such a uniformity of method as admits of little or no variation. Of this kind is, first, the banking trade; secondly, the trade of insurance from fire, and from sea risk and capture in time of war; thirdly, the trade of making and maintaining a navigable cut or canal; and, fourthly, the similar trade of bringing water for the supply of a great city . . .

The joint stock companies, which are established for the public spirited purpose of promoting some particular manufacture, over and above managing their own affairs ill, to the diminution of the general stock of the society, can in other respects scarce ever fail to do more harm than good. Notwithstanding the most upright intentions, the unavoidable partiality of their directors to particular branches of the manufacture, of which the undertakers mislead and impose upon them, is a real discouragement to the rest, and necessarily breaks, more or less, that natural proportion which would otherwise establish itself between judicious industry and profit, and which, to the general industry of the country, is of all encouragements the greatest and the most effectual.[1]

In other words it was Adam Smith's opinion that in a manufacturing industry a corporation could not be well managed and therefore the savings of the investors would be squandered. As for retail or wholesale trade, the operation of a corporation there apparently was unthinkable to Adam Smith. His opinion reflected the relatively undeveloped state of the managerial art in the eighteenth century. It also indicated a skepticism as to the ability of business managers, "notwithstanding the most upright intentions," to observe standards of conduct worthy of confidence and trust.

The readiness with which investors now entrust their savings to corporate managers is indicated by the number of stockholders in corporations, a small sample of which was previously cited. While losses and disappointments sometimes occur, the dire predictions of Adam Smith do not apply generally to present-day corporate management. Methods of management and control have been evolved and standards of executive conduct developed which warrant confidence and trust.

The views voiced by Adam Smith on this and various other topics would not deserve so much attention were it not for the fact that those eighteenth-century views subsequently

[1] Adam Smith, *The Wealth of Nations,* bk. v, chap. I, pt. III, art. I.

had such great influence on the thinking of classical economists and their disciples whose knowledge of current facts did not keep pace with their theorizing. Adam Smith's eighteenth-century suspicion of corporate management is still encountered with some frequency in the middle of the twentieth century despite the developments that meanwhile have taken place. That was the sort of suspicion which apparently was in the mind of the social worker who deemed business executives generally to be rascals.

Avoidance of conflicts of interest

In corporations where the funds with which the enterprises are financed come largely from sources other than the directors and executives, situations may arise which involve potential conflicts of interest between the personal advantage of an executive and the welfare of the company by which he is employed. As experience with this type of relationship has accumulated, however, a code of conduct has evolved which now is quite generally observed. There are exceptions, of course, a few of which presently will be cited, but the nonobservers of the code are looked at more and more askance by other businessmen and by the better informed public. It now is widely realized that an executive not only must avoid abuse of his position of trust, but that he also should avoid any course of action which may give grounds for suspicion that he is guilty of double dealing. Such suspicions lessen confidence in his integrity.

Some of these problems involve potential legal liabilities, but I shall not attempt to deal with their legal aspects — for two reasons. First, I am not qualified to discuss these legal matters. Second, the problems which seem to me to be especially significant are those where the generally acceptable standard of conduct substantially transcends the minimum set by the law.

Commercial bribery is a crude type of improper conduct which has been largely eliminated in this country. Commercial bribery occurs, for example, when an executive in charge of buying accepts a personal gratuity from the vendor as an inducement to place an order with the vendor which otherwise presumably would go to some other potential supplier. The buyer pays a higher price than otherwise would be incurred or suffers some other disadvantage. The conflict of interest arises because the purchasing officer accepts personal gain to the disadvantage of the company by which he is employed. The acceptance of a bribe by a purchasing officer is a violation of trust since it is his responsibility to buy to the best advantage of the company. The vendor who pays a bribe also is guilty of misconduct by becoming a party to an improper transaction. Even in a case where the purchasing company suffers no actual loss from such a transaction, the payment and the acceptance of a bribe are offensive because they create a suspicion of double dealing. Although some petty bribing undoubtedly still occurs, commercial bribery is not generally condoned in American business.

The granting of loans to officers of a company is another delicate matter which may involve a conflict of interest. In September 1930, the executive committee of the board of directors of a well-known company authorized the granting of loans to assist "employees who are in distress because of the stock market situation." The reason for this action, in the words of the stockholders' investigating committee appointed three years later to consider this and other complaints, was as follows: "Many of the officers and employees, including certain directors who were executive officers, were in debt to brokers, banks and others. The collateral was fast becoming insufficient. The collapse of values created distress, which, it was believed, was impairing the efficiency of these officers and employees and thereby of the corporation."

On July 31, 1932, the total loans made under this authorization aggregated $2,545,718, including a loan of $250,000 to the president of the company. With the exception of the loan to the president, all the loans were secured by collateral.

These loans were authorized in order to protect what was believed to be the interests of the company in time of crisis, but they involved a potential conflict of interest, which tacitly was recognized by the president when he directed the secretary of the corporation not to report the authorizing action of the full board of directors. Eventually all the loans were repaid so that the company actually suffered no financial loss, and the company may have benefited from improved performance by officers whose worries were lessened by the loans. Nevertheless these loans smacked of impropriety, and this episode contributed to bring about a forced retirement of the president in 1934. There had been an impairment of confidence in his ability to follow a completely forthright course where his personal interest potentially was in conflict with that of the company. It is to be noted that in this case, as in so many others, it was in a period of great stress that the president's standard of personal conduct was put to the test.

The granting of loans to officers of a corporation under such conditions as those just cited has been a rare occurrence and that particular sort of experience very likely never will be repeated. The example does serve, however, to illustrate what is involved in these conflicts of interest.

Another practice now relatively rare is that of an executive selling property in which he personally is interested to a corporation of which he is an influential officer. Not only may there be legal complications for him in such a deal, but even more important his reputation may thereby be placed at stake. It is not a question of whether the deal is to the advantage or to the disadvantage of the company. The significant question is whether a transaction may give grounds for suspicion of double dealing. An executive who values his standards of conduct carefully eschews situations where his motives may be suspect.

Conflicts of interest involving standards of personal conduct occur, of course, in fields other than business management. In 1950, for example, it was brought out that a member of the United States Senate had received ten thousand dollars for writing a "book" on housing for a house-manufacturing company which was heavily in debt to the Reconstruction Finance Corporation, the company later defaulting on its loan. The senator receiving that payment may have ability to write a book — far be it from me to question a senator's ability to do that — but he seems to have had no particular qualifications as an expert writer on the subject of housing. His critics suspected that his value as an author in that case arose primarily from his influence as a senator. Some critics also expressed surprise that the senator's conduct did not receive more severe condemnation from other members of the Senate.

The foregoing example is only one of a considerable number of situations that have involved questionable standards of conduct in the field of government — federal, state, and local. Without pursuing that subject further, however, suffice it to point out that both in business and in government, situations which give rise to suspicions of double dealing are avoided by men with high standards of conduct.

In business management a somewhat more subtle conflict of interest is involved in nepotism and on this count standards of conduct are not so high as in various other matters. The conflict of interest arises when an executive contemplates having the corporation hire his son or other relative to be placed in a position where he receives compensation greater than his true worth to the company. The executive's family benefits at the expense of the company.

Nepotism is a particularly difficult problem to deal with, because some sons turn out to be abler than their fathers, and a rule against the employment of any relative may work against the best interest of the company. Perhaps the greatest source of difficulty, however, arises out of the inability of the father to evaluate accurately the ability of his son or favorite nephew. Furthermore, even when the father has some inkling that the young man is not of topnotch caliber, the boy's mother probably will not agree. Consequently to lessen turmoil in the family the boy may be given a job for which he is not qualified.

Some years ago the three chief stockholders in a large retail company signed a written agreement among themselves that no son or other near relative of any one of the three should ever be employed by the company. As it turned out, one of the three had an exceptionally able son who took a position in a retail store in another city where he had a distinguished career. The father's company was deprived by the agreement from availing itself of the son's services. Nevertheless, I surmise that the father was content inasmuch as the rule provided some useful protection from other quarters, and he also could derive satisfaction from the independent success achieved by his son.

The public criticism of the bonuses paid to the executives of certain companies has arisen primarily from the suspicion that the executives who were the chief beneficiaries had been largely instrumental in securing adoption of the bonus plans. The subject of executive compensation is to be discussed later, but reference is made to bonus plans here because of the fact that under some conditions they do involve an apparent conflict of interest. Outsiders suspect that the executives have used their influence to put their selfish interest ahead of the welfare of the company by which they are employed.

To sum up, it is fair to assume that most men intend to be honest and faithful to the trust imposed in them. It is so important for an executive, however, to maintain a reputation for integrity and unselfish fulfillment of his responsibilities that many executives have set for themselves standards of conduct which avoid even any appearance of exploitation of their positions for improper personal gain.

Compliance with the law

Compliance with the law raises still other problems of conduct for the business executive, some of which are not easily solved, particularly in periods when business corporations appear to be popular targets for attack by ambitious politicians. We have such a multiplicity of laws, local, state, and federal, that no person can be sufficiently conversant with all of them to enable him to avoid at least occasional transgressions. Then, too, there are serious inconsistencies and conflicts in some of our laws, so that in observing one law a person may break another. And practices long considered legal may suddenly be challenged by some crusading enforcement officer or officious administrative department. Under such conditions there is no certainty of immunity for law-abiding executives.

Confusion and uncertainty have been especially prevalent in recent years in certain segments of the antitrust law field. And at times it almost seems that some of the government officials charged with the enforcement of those laws and some members of Congress have an aversion to having certain of those laws clarified so that they can serve as dependable guides to business conduct. If such be their attitude, it would of course be understandable from a certain point of view. The clearer the law, the fewer the complaints to be issued, the scarcer the opportunities to make political capital in newspaper headlines, and the smaller the staffs to be employed in the enforcement agencies. A bureaucracy thrives on uncertainty and confusion.

From the standpoint of business administration, however, the rules of the game should be made clear in principle, so that executives who are disposed to comply with the law readily can do so. From my experience and observation, it is not fair to assume or imply that business executives generally are seeking to effect combinations in restraint of trade. On the contrary there are a large number who sincerely believe in competition and who would follow the rules if those rules were clear and reasonably free from inconsistencies.

The antitrust laws forbidding agreements and combinations in restraint of trade, which have been in force in the United States since the passage of the Sherman Act in 1890, are basically sound. The United States is the only major industrial country having such laws, and I am convinced that these laws, by preventing the formation of cartels and checking the use of other restrictive devices, have fostered the industrial and economic progress of the country. They have helped to preserve the vigorous competition which generally has characterized American industry, and thereby they have benefited business itself as well as consumers. By maintaining greater opportunities for independence of action they have facilitated effective executive leadership.

There are times, of course, when competition does not look highly attractive to all the participants in the game. Those firms which are having difficulty in maintaining the pace often resort to desperate efforts to remain alive. They cut prices below costs and indulge in other disruptive measures. And their gasping attempts to survive frequently work hardship on their better managed competitors. Such hardships as these, however, are part of the price that we have to pay for being privileged to operate under competitive conditions.

Competition implies that the losers must suffer the penalty of failure. Some of the latter-day amendments to the antitrust laws, however, seem to be inconsistent, at least as they are enforced, with the basic principles of competition. Some of those amendments apparently are aimed at protecting firms which are less competent from having to incur the economic penalties of their ineptness. In order to correct such inconsistencies and also to clarify other provisions of the law, it will be in order in the not distant future to have the whole set of antitrust laws overhauled and revised. There is a major opportunity for leadership in government and business.

Over the last thirty years numerous attempts have been made to set up industrial "codes of ethics," both on a voluntary basis and under government sponsorship, which have aimed at establishing standards of conduct for business management and which also have had legal implications.

The vicissitudes of competition in various distressed industries in the 1920's and early 1930's led to the formulation of such codes for those industries. The code movement culminated in the NRA program inaugurated under government sponsorship in 1933 and virtually terminated with the decision of the Supreme Court in the Schechter case in 1935. Both the earlier voluntary codes and the NRA codes varied in detail between industries, of course, but they had numerous features in common. Although called "codes of ethics," they usually dealt with economic, not ethical, problems. They sought to curb selling below cost, to prevent the guaranteeing of protection to customers against losses from reductions in prices, and to regulate various other trade practices which came under the popular term of "chiseling." In other words they sought to eliminate some of the annoying devices utilized widely in a period of distressful competition. There is still a strong latent desire, I suspect, among a considerable number of businessmen that they be permitted to set up such codes again under government auspices, and if presently we shall encounter another severe business depression, the demand for such codes almost certainly will reappear.

Such codes generally were ineffective and, in my judgment, they are likely to continue to be ineffective in the future, if they are again authorized, unless the antitrust laws are to be abrogated and the germs of a police state planted.

Such a code is difficult to formulate and far more difficult to enforce. In most industries operations are carried on in a variety of ways. The privilege of adopting a different method of operation is one of the advantages and a source of strength for private initiative in business management. A code, however, tends to freeze existing methods and stifle innovations. It tends to be formulated and administered with a view to the safeguarding of vested interests which may be discomfited by innovations. It is not an easy matter to ascertain violations of such a code without recourse to a spy system which readily can develop into an obnoxious police organization. And it is difficult to find sanctions for enforcement which can be applied without virtual nullification of the antitrust laws.

Higher standards of conduct in business management are more likely to be encouraged by clarifying and simplifying existing laws and by the elimination of inconsistencies in the laws now on the books than by the legalizing of such trade prohibitions as commonly have been incorporated in these so-called "codes of ethics." In business as in private life the attainment of really high standards of conduct is achieved not by legislative pronouncement but by voluntary recognition of what is right and decent.

The light of day

For effective and reputable administration the test of an administrative policy or practice is not necessarily whether it will pay or whether it will yield the greatest profit. With broad-gauge management, so far as my observations and experience go, the test of ability to stand the light of day also is widely applied. While a business concern naturally aims to earn a profit in order to justify its economic existence, one that values its reputation aims to observe decent standards of conduct, and a decent standard of conduct usually can stand exposure to the light of day.

In the case of company reports, for example, the executives of many a corporation now seek to furnish as full information to stockholders and potential investors as can be done without jeopardizing the company's competitive position by giving away its hand. It is true that many stockholders may not examine a company's report with care, but some do examine it thoroughly, and their examination suffices to put the report to test.

In the marketing field there has been a spread during the last forty years of the policy of selling on openly announced terms and prices, with no secret concessions to favored customers. Such a policy is still far from being universally accepted; in some instances the radical changes taking place in the field of distribution have furnished excuses for a company's nonadoption of such a policy. Nevertheless several companies with whose affairs I am intimately acquainted have long sold their products only on openly announced terms and prices, without secret concessions, and they not only have established notable reputations for integrity but their executives have gained certain comforts of mind from adherence to that clear-cut policy.

In other cases companies conduct their sales operations

frankly on a horse-trading basis, dickering on each transaction. When it is understood by a company's customers that every sale is subject to price negotiation, with no pretense at treating all customers alike beyond permitting them to engage in dickering, that too is an open and aboveboard policy. The cases of questionable standards of conduct arise where companies pretend to have definite policies but then do not adhere to them.

In situations involving potential conflicts of interest for directors or executives of a company, such as those to which reference previously was made, ability to stand the light of day is a useful test for application. Arrangements or dealings with directors or executives which cannot readily stand up under full exposure are not wisely undertaken.

As the foregoing examples illustrate, there are wide ranges of situations in which the adoption of practices and policies which can bear exposure to the light of day furnishes a useful guide for a standard of executive conduct. It is not to be expected, of course, that such a test will be universally acceptable. In the business field the number of firms is so large and the background, concepts, and character of their owners and executives are so diverse that it is not reasonable to believe that all the shortsightedness, narrow selfishness, and even the brazenness of the heads of some firms can be overcome by any one device. There are no such simple, easy means of elevating the standards of such a large and diverse segment of the human race.

As is exemplified in numerous corporations, however, these situations do afford especially significant opportunities for leadership. As their experience shows, the light-of-day test does accomplish several things. It promotes improved understanding and therefore better relationship with stockholders, customers, and the public at large. It tends to inspire confidence and thus to strengthen the morale of the whole organization. Not least in significance is the effect on the executive himself. When he accepts such a test for a standard of conduct his whole thinking is conditioned thereby and his outlook broadened. Finally the observance of such a test sets an example which a growing number of executives follow.

The recognition of the light-of-day test for standards of executive conduct is essentially an educational development. The spread of such recognition takes time, because, as I have remarked before, the educational process is a slow process. Leadership by example, however, contributes to progress toward higher standards of conduct.

XII

Rewards of Management

The job of an executive, as has been indicated, involves the making of decisions on a diversity of problems and the assumption of focal responsibilities. He is responsible for the selection, instruction, and guidance of his lieutenants; for securing efficient teamwork; for assuring effective communication and control within the organization; for being prepared to deal with a wide variety of operating problems on which lieutenants seek guidance and advice; for exercising foresight to meet changing conditions; for strategic timing of administrative action; for building the morale of the organization; and for taking on various extracurricular activities in the interest of the enterprise of which he is in charge.

These tasks call for a scarce combination of abilities. They involve an ability to understand people — to size them up, to judge their talents and their character, to sense their motives, and to comprehend how to stimulate them to effective action. These tasks also involve the exercise of mature judgment in dealing with such a variety of problems. They require courage to act and to act promptly; one of the main tests of executive competency, in fact, is the courage to act decisively in an emergency. The courage to act also requires the courage to make mistakes and to admit that mistakes have been made when they do occur; with all the decisions that must be reached, often on short notice and with few facts available, a perfect batting average is humanly inconceivable. These tasks also call for imagination; new problems must have new answers; new conditions offer new opportunities to those who have the imagination as well as the courage to grasp them. Along with imagination and decisiveness in action must go resourcefulness — an ability to find practical means for carrying out the decisions.

In business administration, it is advantageous for a top executive to have some familiarity with a variety of techniques, such as factory operation, engineering, marketing, finance, and accounting, even though he is not a specialist in any one of them. If he has such a familiarity, it is easier for him to comprehend the implications of some of the problems which come to his desk for decision.

Then, too, an executive needs to have a multiple-track mind with rapid switching facilities. He must be switching his attention continually from one subject to another, often without any advance notice as to what is coming next, and unless he can make the necessary mental adjustments almost instantaneously, he becomes lost in a maze.

Moral stamina also is needed — for making courageous decisions, for enduring criticism, and for adhering to a course of action which may be misunderstood by outsiders and which may be temporarily unpopular.

The stresses and strains of leadership, furthermore, tax physical endurance. The burden of decision-making has wracked the nervous and digestive systems of many an executive.

As the directors of numerous corporations have discovered when they have had occasion to fill executive vacancies, the supply of topnotch executive talent is thin. The number of persons available who can endure the mental and physical wear and tear of executive responsibility and who also possess the variety of talents needed for executive leadership usually is quite limited. The supply of executive ability available, moreover, cannot be augmented substantially merely by raising the price paid for that type of service. During the last generation we have learned something about how to train men for executive work, provided they have the inherent qualifications, but as yet we know nothing about how to breed men with those qualifications and I suspect that we never will solve that enigma.

Monetary rewards

The rewards for executive achievement are in part monetary and in part nonmonetary. Let us consider first the monetary rewards.

The size of an executive's salary has become a topic for widespread public discussion within the last fifty years. So long as a large majority of our business enterprises were operated by executives who were proprietors, partners, or dominant stockholders there was little public concern over executive salaries. In those enterprises, furthermore, the executive-proprietors often used substantial portions of the earnings for expanding operations so that much of their reward came in the form of capital enhancement rather than as salary. Nowadays it also is a common practice to finance expansion of operations extensively by the reinvestment of earnings, but the gain therefrom accrues to the stockholders, and in the large, widely owned corporations the executives typically own only small fractions of the stock. For them reinvestment of corporate earnings is not an effective substitute for salary payments.

In addition to the change in ownership-executive relations during the last half century, a social philosophy which has looked askance at large monetary rewards for executives seems to have become more prevalent. I am not prepared to make any flat-footed statements regarding the spread of that philosophy, which has manifested itself in various other ways beside the criticism of executive salaries, but it appears to me that it has gained support, as such movements often do, from two rather diametrically opposed sources. It has been the American frontier tradition to consider one man as good as another, and that inbred attitude leads many a man with modest income and especially a man with mediocre ability to doubt that any person can render services in business management worth $100,000 a year, much less several times that amount. That is an individualistic point of view. Another group of persons, including some enabled to live a life of ease as the beneficiaries of business profits, have been infected by Marxian doctrines and espouse something approaching equalitarianism for executive compensation. The latter group loses no opportunity, of course, for attempting to undermine private enterprise.

It is interesting, although perhaps not enlightening, to note the contrast in public attitudes toward the salaries of highly paid moving-picture actors or radio entertainers, for example, and those of corporation executives. I do not mean to imply that any valid comparison can be made between the services rendered by actors and by executives. They are, of course, in noncompeting groups. But to me it is at least interesting that the popularity of a moving-picture star or a radio entertainer seems to be enhanced by publication of his almost fabulous income, whereas news of the payment of a similar amount to a corporation executive would be likely to engender criticism. In this day and age, just as in declining years of the Roman Empire, it is glamour which catches the public fancy. As certain experiences have shown only too painfully, however, a glamorous corporation executive is more likely to be a handicap than an asset to any company of which he is the head.

At this point, lest I be misunderstood, let me hasten to state that I am not seeking to arouse sympathy for poor, underpaid executives. If any of them feel that they are salary martyrs, let them try their hand at radio announcing or possibly become college professors. Let me add, furthermore, that some business executives are overpaid. Occasionally a suave stuffed shirt lands a sinecure. But similar mistakes also occur in every field of activity with which I am acquainted.

Since there is no established market rate or approximate market rate for such services,[1] the problem of determining the salary to be paid to an executive is a perplexing one. As has been pointed out, the executive's job calls for a scarce combination of abilities. Some of the most significant results of competent administration, moreover, are not immediately apparent. The recruiting and coaching of an able staff, the formulation of sound policies, and the adaptation of a company's affairs to changing conditions all take time. Consequently the value of an executive's services, unless he be thoroughly incompetent, can be judged only on the results attained over a period of years. Then, too, a competent executive is the head of a team. A good leader succeeds in securing teamwork, thereby enabling the other members of the team to accomplish more. But how much of this greater achievement is to be credited to the leader? It is a joint product.

With such a thin supply of talent available and with such complexities inherent in the evaluation of an executive job, it is small wonder that executive salaries cover a wide range.

When an executive vacancy is to be filled, the salary offered must be sufficient to attract a man capable of handling the job. If such a salary cannot be afforded, the enterprise

[1] For evidence regarding the range of executive salaries, see John C. Baker, "Payments to Senior Corporation Executives," *Quarterly Journal of Economics* (February 1945), pp. 170–184.

is not economically sound. Any business enterprise which cannot afford competent management has no justification to be in existence. Poor management is dear at any price and good management may be cheap even at a high salary.

When a new executive is to be hired from outside the company, the salary offered him must be high enough to induce him to make the shift from his current business position or professional activity. There is some competition between jobs which enters into the determination of salaries.

When a top executive vacancy is filled by promotion from within the company's ranks, the new appointee normally receives an increase in salary. In business I never have encountered a procedure such as occurred in a university with which I was connected briefly many years ago. One of the instructors, whose salary was $1,500 a year, was due for a promotion. He also was engaged to be married and had set the date for the wedding. When the president of the university called him in for his interview, the president gave the instructor the choice of two alternatives. He could continue as "instructor" with an increase of $300 a year in salary or he could have a promotion to an assistant professorship at no increase in salary. He supinely took the title. Recently I have been amazed to learn of somewhat similar deals in another university.

As I stated, however, in business a promotion in rank usually carries with it an increase in compensation. The top salaries thus bear some relation to those in the middle management group, and the latter, in turn, are related to the salaries and wages of people further down the scale.

Thus, when a top executive vacancy is to be filled, the amount that has to be paid to induce a prospect to give up his old position for the new job and the salary scale for other officers of the company provide a few rough guides to help in determining the rate of compensation.

Since the starting salary for an executive may be subject to increases if the company prospers under his management, the salary problem is not necessarily settled once and for all when the rate of compensation of a new executive has been fixed. But in determining the increases in salary, if any, to be granted to a veteran executive a variety of considerations, some of them analogous to the ones just cited, enter into the deliberation of the board of directors. Reward for services rendered is the most substantial ground for granting increases in executive salaries. Even though the value of an executive's services cannot be measured precisely, observation of his performance over a period of years indicates whether he merits additional compensation.

Another factor which may come up for consideration is that of incentive payments. The question of whether frequent increases in salary are necessary to induce an executive to put forth his best efforts is a moot one. And the answer probably depends in part on the executive himself. The incentive aspects of executive compensation, in my opinion, tend to be overstressed, but undoubtedly there are executives whose zest for financial gain is so strong that their managerial talents are stimulated by the bait of incentive compensation. More will be said on this topic shortly.

In some instances I am convinced that increases in salary are granted primarily in emulation of other companies. The president of one company likes to feel that he is as big a man as the president of some other company, and to him this importance is measured by the salary which he receives. If his rival, Mr. Jones, receives an increase in salary, he cannot be happy without a similar increase, and oftentimes the board of directors, I judge, acquiesces with that view. Compensation in some instances thus becomes a yardstick of esteem.

So far as I can tell, there is no simple formula to be applied which will determine more or less automatically what the salary of a particular executive should be. I know that such a formula frequently is sought but I doubt if one can be found.

In the absence of a formula the directors have to arrive at salary decisions by the exercise of judgment. As already has been indicated, some of the major factors which properly enter into salary decisions are the following:

(1) The actual and potential earnings of the company and its financial condition. These items place an upper limit in some companies on what salaries they can afford to pay to their executives. In many instances, however, a company is so strong and so prosperous that this limit has no practical significance.

(2) The scale of salaries in the organization. The president normally receives a larger salary than that which is paid to a department head. That is not universally true, because sometimes a department head is such a skilled specialist that he is paid at a higher rate than his boss. Nevertheless the scale of salaries in the organization ordinarily is one of the factors which enter into the fixing of the top executive's salary.

(3) Competition. How much is it necessary to offer a competent man to induce him to take the job? And after he has achieved a reputation, how much is it necessary to pay him to avoid having him hired away by some other company? Companies which are in the market for new executives are continually scouting the field for likely prospects who already have demonstrated their competency.

(4) Enabling an executive to live in such comfort as the tax laws permit. The scale on which an executive lives properly is a matter of concern to the directors of the company by which he is employed. He usually has occasion to do some entertaining of business associates and customers, and in

such matters it is not to the advantage of the company to encourage niggardliness. And in many community affairs the scale of contributions by an executive not only affects his personal standing but also is of concern to the company which pays his salary.

(5) Stockholder and employee relations and attitude of the general public. How much an executive's services are worth to a company, even if that figure could be accurately ascertained, is not necessarily a dominant factor in salary determination. It is conceivable that an executive's services might be worth $1,000,000 a year to a company, but that does not mean that it would be wise policy to pay him that amount. There is one large company, for example, organized half a century ago, which has shown respectable earnings only in war years or in periods of boom activity. If an executive could be found who could revamp that company's organization, correct some of its policies, develop a new *esprit de corps,* and effect such other changes as might be called for, his services probably could be worth $1,000,000 a year to the stockholders of the company, and the employees also would be better off. Nevertheless, if an executive could be found competent to achieve such results, he also almost certainly would be smart enough not to accept a salary of that amount. He would realize how vaguely his services would be understood by many stockholders and by many employees and how that lack of understanding would lead to criticisms and bickerings which would hamper, if not cripple, his administrative activities.

Take another specific instance. In March 1943, the board of directors of Standard Oil Company (New Jersey) adopted a resolution: "That, during the period in which this country is engaged in the present war no Director or Officer shall receive a salary in excess of $100,000 annually." [2] The Standard

[2] John C. Baker, *Directors and Their Functions,* p. 103.

Oil Company (New Jersey) is one of the largest corporations in the world and a thoroughly prosperous one. That action in limiting executive salaries was not occasioned by financial necessity but, I judge, by considerations of public policy. Numerous other companies, I am confident, have been activated by similar considerations in fixing executive salaries at amounts which were not fully commensurate with services rendered. Adam Smith presumably would be as greatly surprised by such actions as he would by the telephone, the radio, and various other modern achievements.

Executive bonus plans

Since incentive wage systems for factory employees and various bonus plans for salesmen have worked out successfully, it has been inferred in some companies that bonus plans will have an analogously stimulating effect on executives. I will grant, of course, that executives are not of greatly different breed, but at the same time I venture to raise a question as to whether the conditions of executive work warrant drawing such an analogy. Although executive bonus plans may be susceptible of justification on other grounds, I am skeptical as to the worth of most of such plans from an incentive standpoint.

An executive bonus plan ordinarily provides for computation of the bonus on an annual basis. The theory of a bonus calls for prompt reward for efforts expended. The computation of a bonus on the basis of annual results, however, is a major element of weakness in such a plan. Corporate earnings and executive effort do not correlate closely on an annual basis.

For many years the late Charles M. Schwab, Chairman of the Board of Directors of Bethlehem Steel Corporation, was an ardent believer in a profit sharing or bonus plan for executives. In a letter to stockholders in March 1931 on "The Bethlehem Bonus System" Mr. Schwab stated: "Bethlehem has made wide use of piece rates, tonnage rates, premiums and group incentive plans for wage earners, and various forms of incentive payments for supervisors and others in the ranks of management. Do so much and you get so much; do more and you get more — that is the essence of the system." Mr. Schwab, himself, it should be noted, as chairman of the board of directors did not receive any bonus. He administered the plan without himself being a beneficiary.

The statistics given in an appendix to Mr. Schwab's letter showed a close correlation between executive bonus payments and general business conditions. The president of the company, for example, received a fixed salary of $12,000 a year. In 1919 his bonus was $782,031; and in 1920, $799,802; 1921, $388,545; and in 1922, $231,790. These bonus payments were related to the company's earnings, and the fluctuations in earnings in the years just cited were caused primarily by changes in business conditions. In 1928 the president's bonus went up to $831,445 and in 1929 to $1,623,753, a rise to be attributed to the general business boom rather than to the extra effort exerted by executives of the company.

The Bethlehem experience is ancient history now, its executive bonus plan having been radically modified in 1931. But that experience does illustrate a point common to many executive bonus plans. The amount of bonus paid commonly is governed by general business conditions as reflected in corporate earnings rather than by executive effort. It would be ridiculous, in fact, to assume that the president of Bethlehem Steel Corporation worked five times as hard or five times as effectively in 1929 as in 1922, which would have had to be the case if his compensation were strictly commensurate with the services which he rendered. As a matter of fact, the executives of a corporation probably work harder and certainly undergo much more severe strains in periods of depression than they do in periods of prosperity. The Bethlehem experience may be ancient history for that company, but the same principle is inherent in numerous other executive bonus plans currently in operation.

If the principle of "do so much and you get so much; do more and you get more" were to be applied in a fully logical manner in these executive bonus plans, an executive should be expected to make a contribution to the company's treasury whenever the company goes into the red. If he is responsible for the earnings in boom years, he also presumably should be held responsible for losses in bad years. If a profit-sharing or bonus plan is to be supported as an incentive device, it logically should provide for a sharing of losses as well as a sharing of profits. So far as I am aware, however, the advocates of profit sharing and executive bonus plans have not been to that degree logical.

An executive bonus plan in some instances has had definitely undesirable results. An annual bonus for executives may encourage a short-run point of view rather than the long-range welfare of the company, and thereby lead to a conflict between the interest of the executives of the company and that of its stockholders and of its other employees.

In one such instance which came to my attention a company, which had a bonus plan for executives, delivered a shipment of merchandise to a customer which proved to be unsatisfactory. Technically the company may not have been liable for the defects in the goods, but the customer complained and had strong grounds for seeking restitution. The amount involved was $500,000. The customer was a large buyer, and his future patronage would be jeopardized by rejection of his request for restitution. The executives of the company, nevertheless, decided against making any adjustment with the customer, and some of the executives during their discussion of the case stated frankly that they were more interested in their current bonuses than they were in the future goodwill of the company.

In another instance the executives of a company which had an executive bonus plan launched a program which would have increased their bonuses substantially, if it had succeeded, but which actually led instead to a loss of upwards of $1,000,000 to the company. The bonus plan encouraged the executives to follow a speculative course where they would share in any profits that resulted but not participate in the loss if it failed.

An executive bonus, as has been pointed out, usually is governed by the company's annual earnings. Some of the more important executive decisions made during that year will not bear fruit, however, for several years to come. A period of time is required for putting a new policy into effect and for it to bear results. It is likely to require several years for the successful introduction of a new product, for example, even after the technical research has been completed. During that period of introduction, the development and promotional costs may be substantially greater than the earnings on the new product. That is a commonplace experience, and the same goes for numerous other types of executive problems. The answer to the objection just raised is likely to be that of course an executive will be broad-minded enough to look ahead and not sacrifice future opportunity for immediate gain, an answer which in effect negates the incentive basis on which executive bonuses commonly are supported. To the extent that such bonuses do encourage the seeking of immediate rewards at the expense of foresighted programming for the long run, they work to the disadvantage of the company.

From my observation it appears to me that irrespective of methods of executive compensation, there tends to be too much shortsightedness in corporate management, and any scheme, such as executive bonuses, which tends to accentuate such shortsightedness is in itself a shortsighted policy. Furthermore, if a person is of a type that needs a bonus incentive to induce him to put forth his full efforts for the company by which he is employed, it seems to me to be fairly certain that he is likely to yield to the temptation to cash in on short-run gains even when they mean long-run sacrifices to the company.

In passing, finally, reference probably should be made to stockholder criticism of some executive bonus plans. The critics may not be numerous. They may not be impelled by the highest motives in making their complaints. And those complaints may be quite unjustified. Nevertheless there seems to be a rather widespread suspicion that some executives have used the influence of their positions to secure the adoption of plans under which they have received large bonuses.

There is something to be said for executive bonuses on grounds other than direct incentive rewards. Such a plan may lessen the fixed salary charge on a company and thus yield greater flexibility. In a period of low earnings it is much easier psychologically to reduce an executive's bonus than it is to cut his salary. And in years of good company earnings a liberal bonus can be paid without its being a severe strain on a company's finances. If the bonus be a modest one, not a high percentage of an executive's salary, such an arrangement probably has considerable merit.

A large number of companies, including many prosperous ones, pay their executives solely on a salary basis. Since the results of executive leadership can be judged fairly only by averaging the good years with the lean ones and by averaging in also other factors which show their effects in periods of years rather than of months, the salary type of reward has been deemed most useful for executive compensation in many business corporations. An executive may fairly expect that a periodic appraisal of his services will be made by the board of directors. If such an appraisal is made, with appropriate increases when circumstances warrant them, an executive is offered the sort of incentive which should be most conducive to broad-visioned management. There is nothing very spectacular or glamorous in the salary type of compensation, but that well may be one of its greatest merits for many corporations.

An opportunity to acquire a proprietary interest in the enterprise of which he is in charge is another form of monetary incentive for an executive. Under some conditions that doubtless is a strong incentive, especially in small enterprises. Nevertheless, in my judgment, the proprietary incentive for executives, and incidentally also for other employees, frequently is overestimated. The purpose in giving an executive an opportunity to acquire a proprietary interest is to stimulate effort both for the sake of immediate gain and also for building an estate. Income tax laws being what they are, opportunities to build estates for their heirs count heavily with most executives.

Executive achievement, however, requires far more than mere industriousness, and executive competency is not created merely by possession of a proprietary interest. The supply of able executives cannot be increased simply by affording greater opportunities for the acquiring of proprietary interest in a corporation any more than by merely raising the price paid for executive services. Executive competency is the product of innate ability and long-cultivated talents more than of the method of compensation for services. One does not have to look far in the business field to observe numerous instances in which enterprises run by their owners are not successful, or, on the other hand, to note companies which are ably managed by executives who have no substantial share in the ownership of the enterprises of which they are in charge. There is no magic in a proprietary interest.

In making these observations with regard to incentives, I am fully aware that there are dangers in generalization, for different individuals react quite differently to monetary incentives. Some men tend to stagnate, if they feel that they have reached the ceiling of monetary rewards. Others keep up the pace.

To sum up, an executive should be worth his hire and he should receive fair compensation for services rendered. But the problem of obtaining good management is not primarily one of finding a formula for financial compensation. A competent executive must be paid enough to induce him to assume the responsibilities and to carry the burden of the job. If the enterprise is a successful one over a period of years, he properly may expect to receive recognition for his share in its success by being granted an increased monetary reward. He can be more effective as an executive, however, if he is not the beneficiary of any plan which inherently produces a conflict between his own self-interest and the interests of the company as a whole, or which gives ground for suspicion that he is using a dominating position "to feather his own nest." For real executive achievement consideration of the interests of the whole enterprise must be put ahead of the interests of any one individual. The welfare of the company is placed first.

Nonmonetary rewards

In addition to his financial compensation, a successful business executive usually receives other rewards, such as personal prestige and the satisfaction of having handled a job with proficiency. This is what the economists call "psychic income." It is the sort of sustenance on which we professors and our families thrive. Psychic income, in fact, is one thing which professors and business executives have in common, albeit in quite different proportions.

In his autobiography[3] Andrew Carnegie cites an example of youthful psychic income, although he did not call it by any such dignified name and even grossly disparaged its significance. Mr. Carnegie related how he persuaded other boys to gather food for his rabbits, "the compensation being that the young rabbits, when they came, should be named after them." Then he went on to state: "My conscience reproves me today, looking back, when I think of the hard bargain I drove with my young playmates, many of whom were content to gather dandelions and clover for a whole season with me, conditioned upon this unique reward — the poorest return ever made to labor. Alas! What else had I to offer them! Not a penny."

Mr. Carnegie still further added: "I treasure the remembrance of this plan as the earliest evidence of organizing power upon the development of which my material success in life has hung — a success not to be attributed to what I have known or done myself, but to the faculty of knowing and choosing others who did know better than myself. Precious knowledge this for any man to possess. I did not understand steam machinery, but I tried to understand that much more complicated piece of mechanism — man."

Mr. Carnegie might well have observed, too, that one who would understand men should understand boys.

The attainment of a top executive position in itself yields a particularly gratifying reward, irrespective of the financial emoluments of the job. If the company is a prosperous one, the recognition which almost automatically is accorded to its executive in the industry and trade circles of which the company is a member and in the community at large is highly

[3] *Autobiography of Andrew Carnegie* (Boston: Houghton Mifflin, 1920), p. 24.

gratifying to most men. Continued prosperity of the company tends to enhance the prestige of its executives and thus add to their satisfaction. The prestige which comes from demonstrated accomplishment is a reward for efforts expended in the past and an incentive to greater accomplishments in the future.

It is because of the prestige of his position and of his achievements that many of the demands are made on an executive to participate in extracurricular activities. Those activities often are a heavy burden for him, but from some of them he is likely to reap certain of his most stimulating rewards, such as promotion of the public welfare. By participating in these activities, furthermore, he is admitted to groups of other successful executives. Admission to those groups is a tacit and rewarding recognition of his achievements.

An executive cannot always attain prestige or hold it if he does attain it. He may lose it. And loss of prestige, for whatever reason it occurs, can be a grievous blow. Many a man who can take a financial loss with a grin cannot endure a loss of prestige. Hence, in a negative sort of a way, fear of a loss of prestige serves as a spur to executive effort.

Another nonmonetary reward is the satisfaction which an executive receives from doing a job well, from demonstrating that he is proficient in his administrative capacity. Proficiency on the job, I am convinced from my observations, is one of the most universal of satisfactions. It is enjoyed not only by executives in business and in other types of organizations; it also is manifested by workmen in all sorts of occupations, by cooks, by athletes, and not least by fishermen. The thrill of demonstrated proficiency is a powerful reward; a person, be he high or low in the scale of employment, does a substantially better job when he derives the satisfaction of personal proficiency and does not think merely of his pay envelope.

Personal proficiency is a subject about which a capable executive usually does not do much talking. His satisfaction is indicated rather by a certain self-assurance in manner, by his casual comments on the problems with which he has to deal, by a certain zest in his conversation, and by a revealing gleam in his eye. These manifestations are indicative of the depth of the satisfaction.

Still another nonmonetary reward for a competent executive is the satisfaction which he derives from rendering service to other participants in the enterprise and to the community in which the enterprise operates. As I write this paragraph I can see a benevolent old gentleman standing at the head of a large luncheon table, or rather series of tables, at which were seated a group of executives, staff members, and stockholders. The old gentleman was chairman of the board of directors of the company. Under his guidance over a period of fifty years, the company had grown and prospered, to the benefit of the employees, the officers, the stockholders, and the customers. From the remarks which the old gentleman made it was apparent that he was deeply gratified to have been able to guide the development of an enterprise from which so many persons had benefited. He had prospered financially but the enhancing of the welfare of the whole group had been one of his most cherished rewards.

Although these nonmonetary rewards are not measurable, or at least never have been measured, nevertheless they have a powerful influence on executive leaders. They induce numerous executives to continue to work at top speed even when those executives undoubtedly could hold their jobs even if they slackened their efforts somewhat. It is such incentives as these which induce numerous executives to keep up their steam even when they have no expectation of receiving an increase in monetary compensation. These considerations also explain why sometimes a man chooses to remain in one position when he has an opportunity to move to another one at substantially higher pay.

Why is the supply of top executives so thin?

In view of the rewards attainable for management, both monetary and nonmonetary, the question may well be raised as to why the supply of competent top executives is so thin. I am not prepared to make a comprehensive answer to that question, but I will venture to suggest a couple of reasons. These reasons do not include income tax complications. Heavy income taxation may discourage initiative and tend to cause a lessening of the supply of executive candidates at some time in the future, but I doubt if it has had any such effect as yet.

Since both of the reasons that I am venturing to suggest have been referred to at earlier points, my mention of them here is primarily for purposes of emphasis.

The first of the reasons to be suggested is the dearth of men with multiple-track minds, men who can switch with facility from one problem to another and still maintain a reasonably high batting average on the variety of decisions to be made. Lower in the ranks it is difficult to find men with even two-track minds. Several years ago, for example, a large, well-known, and highly prosperous company added a new product to the line. Its former products had been distributed intensively through wholesalers to a large number of retail stores. The new product was of a different type. The inventory assortment required for consumer satisfaction was such that only a limited number of carefully selected retail stores could afford to carry that line. The company, however, attempted to have its regular sales force distribute the new product as well as the old line, without realizing that selling on a selected distribution program is quite a different task from selling for intensive distribution. The sales officers and the salesmen, who continued to sell the older products, never did succeed in handling the new line successfully. They did not have two-track minds. Eventually the company discontinued the new product, having lost upwards of $1,000,000 in the venture.

In factory work, I understand, it typically is found necessary to segregate special-order work from standard production, one of the complications being the inability of a supervisory force to shift its thinking continually and rapidly from one type of work to the other.

As these examples suggest, few people have even two-track minds, with adequate switching facilities. Far fewer have the type of multiple-track mind needed for competent topside administration.

The other reason for the thinness of the supply of competent top executives is the reluctance of so many persons to assume responsibilities. This trait also is to be observed at all stages in an organization. Of course everyone would like to have a larger income, but it is not correct to assume that every employee is ambitious to rise in the ranks of management. Many an employee shrinks or shies away from taking responsibility.

This shrinking from the assumption of responsibility, I judge, comes in part from inertia, from laziness if you will, from a desire to avoid mental effort. To an even greater extent it seems to come from a lack of self-confidence and from fear — the fear of making mistakes and the fear of being shown up as lacking in proficiency. A good deal of animal comfort, furthermore, is to be derived from merely being able to live a life of well-established routine, with freedom from the bother of making up one's mind too frequently on too many problems. The freedom of routine is one of the rewards for not being ambitious.

Many a time the chief executive of a business enterprise,

beset and bedeviled by a multitude of harassing problems, may well envy those who have shunned responsibility and who consequently can go to bed complacently each night.

Basically, I suppose, the reasons for the dearth of really first-rate executives are much the same as the inscrutable reasons for the dearth of outstanding performers in practically every type of human endeavor. However adequate or however inadequate their scale of compensation may be, the number of persons richly endowed with creative power is everywhere small.

XIII

Providing for Retirement

Sooner or later every executive must of necessity face either retirement or replacement. That is an inescapable edict of Father Time. The continued welfare of an enterprise is more likely to be assured if some provision is made in advance for the retirement of its executive leader and for the choice of his successor. This should be an obvious truth. Despite the obviousness of that truth, however, provision for retirement is by no means a universal practice, and when provision is made, retirement is accepted only with reluctance by a considerable number of those retired.

This subject of retirement is one of especial poignancy for me personally at this time. As I am writing this chapter, I am slightly over sixty-six years old. Under the university's statutes I normally would have gone into retirement three weeks ago. But, because of circumstances entirely beyond my control, my retirement has been deferred for a couple of years by the university's governing boards. I was fully prepared to retire and the writing of this book was to have been one of the first items on my schedule in retirement. When I learned that my retirement was to be deferred, I decided to go ahead with the writing on somewhat of a piecemeal basis so that I might still have time left for some of the other things which I am looking forward to doing when at last there is leisure for them. Later in this chapter I shall take the liberty of saying something more about my personal experiences in preparing for retirement, but at this point I merely wish to disclose the fact that my views on retirement may not be wholly objective ones. My situation is not fully comparable to that of a business executive, to be sure, but I am observing that we do have some things in common. Agewise, at least, I am in a position to look sympathetically at the problems of executives preparing to turn over the reins of management to someone else.

In retrospect I have noted that just about the time that I turned sixty the subject of retirement began to crop up more and more frequently in my casual conversations with business and professional men of my own and an earlier vintage. A little later younger men occasionally made an indirect or hesitating reference to my impending retirement. Some of these conversations and accompanying observations have been quite revealing to me, and I believe that they serve to give something of the general atmosphere of executive retirement.

One of my intimate old friends who has retired was president of a bank in which he is a large stockholder. He decided voluntarily and willingly, on his own initiative, to retire when he was about sixty-three years old. He has continued to serve as a member of the board of directors of the bank, but devotes only a small amount of time to that task. He does some gardening, travels with his wife occasionally, plays bridge, and just loafs around. He is enjoying himself thoroughly in retirement. Even in his college days he was an adept at loafing around, and he has not lost his knack.

About six years ago I happened to mention to another old acquaintance, a corporation lawyer, then about seventy-two years of age, that I was making plans for retirement. He asked me what on earth I would do if I had to retire. He went on to remark that were he to retire he would be completely lost. He would not know what to do with himself. In subsequent casual conversations I have found that he still has a great dread of retirement and a dislike for all retirement plans. He has ample financial means to support himself in retirement but he cannot make the psychological adjustment. His is a particularly typical case.

Another example which was cited to me in one of these conversations was that of an old sea captain down in Maine. My friend met the sea captain just after the captain had come ashore to retire at the age of sixty-five, and my friend remarked: "Well, captain, now that you have come ashore to retire, I suppose you are going to enjoy life." "Enjoy life," growled the captain, "Hell, I've come ashore to die." And within a year he was dead.

One of my academic associates, in his early fifties, cannot bear to participate in any discussion of retirement. For him, as for numerous other professional and business men, the subject is such a morbid one that he just does not want to talk about it or to hear anyone else discuss it.

A final example is that of a business acquaintance who is president of a subsidiary of a large corporation. This executive is three years away from retirement, and yet he has made no plans for retiring. Only recently he remarked: "If I retire, I shall have some problems of adjustment." He is still thinking in terms of "if I retire," rather than "when I retire." He knows that he will have to retire, but psychologically he is wholly unprepared for retirement. For him, furthermore, as for most of us, it is difficult to admit that someone else may be able to handle the job as well as he is handling it. We tend to think of ourselves as being irreplaceable. During the last forty years I have failed to note any specific case of irreplaceability of an executive, in either the business or the academic field. And yet we like to pride ourselves on being indispensable.

In my casual conversations over the last half-dozen years with men verging on retirement, I have noted a reluctance to retire or a fatalistic acceptance of retirement as an inescapable catastrophe being manifested with especial frequency. The increased longevity in the current era tends to prolong the period after retirement, but I sometimes feel that by some of my friends greater longevity at least in retirement will be regretted rather than welcomed.

The foregoing instances, which could be multiplied many times over, illustrate how frequently a man is emotionally averse to retirement when his turn comes. A pension plan helps to remove the economic objection to retirement but it does not eliminate and seldom lessens the emotional resistance. This reluctance to let go of the reins of management and to face retirement appears to me to be one of the main reasons why so frequently inadequate provisions are made for succession in management, even when a retirement program has been set up.

The executive's responsibility

From an economic and social point of view one of the major advantages in the corporate form of business organization is its potential permanency. A corporation can continue to live far beyond the span of life of its founders. Executives can come and executives can go but the company may remain in existence provided it serves a purpose sufficiently useful to attract a sustaining patronage and provided timely arrangements are made for continuing leadership.

An executive who devotes a substantial portion of his life to the management of a prosperous enterprise naturally has a keen interest in having its success continue after his term of service ends. In fact an encouraging outlook for the continued prosperity of the enterprise commonly is one of the satisfactions which reward him for his efforts. But then a conflict of motives comes in. The executive's desire to build for the future of the company is insidiously at variance with his reluctance to make adequate provisions for stepping aside in favor of a new leader.

The continued success of a business concern after the retirement of a chief executive depends, of course, on a variety of factors, such as the condition of the physical plant, the products or services developed, the market established, and the financial strength built up. It also depends on the base which has been laid in the selection and training of the administrative personnel and in the development of effective policies. Continued success also hinges on the choice of a successor and on the circumstances under which the successor takes over the responsibility for leadership. A new executive must himself secure acceptance of his leadership, but the way can be made smoother for him and the continued prosperity of the enterprise given greater assurance if adequate provisions are made for his succession to office. Arrangements for succession thus are an essential feature of preparation for retirement.

The responsibilities of an executive in getting ready to retire seem to me to be twofold: (1) setting the administrative house in order, and (2) facilitating the selection and induction of his successor.

By setting the administrative house in order I mean cleaning up messy policy situations, correcting any unwholesome operating conditions that may exist, and straightening out administrative personnel tangles. In other words, if there are unpleasant tasks to be performed, the retiring executive can render an especially useful service to the company by performing as many of those unpleasant tasks as possible, in order to make the path of his successor that much smoother. I realize that it is asking a great deal of a retiring executive to expect him to sacrifice his personal comfort and perhaps certain friendly relationships within and without the organization in order to lighten the burden of his successor. But executive achievement often requires self-sacrifice. In fact a willingness to undergo self-sacrifice is a characteristic which particularly commends a leader to his associates, and that self-sacrifice continues into retirement.

In preparing for retirement, to refer to the second point mentioned above, an executive also has a responsibility to facilitate the selection and induction of his successor. The actual choice of a new chief executive is a prerogative of the board of directors of a corporation.[1] The retiring executive, however, can facilitate the work of the board in choosing and installing his successor.

The opportunity for an executive to use his influence to have a board of directors so constituted that it will render the maximum aid to his successor is illustrated by the following rather extreme example. In the early 1930's the president, who was also the largest stockholder, of a moderately sized company decided to retire. He brought in a man from outside as his successor. The board of directors was made up entirely of officers of the company. The concern had been highly prosperous for many years, but just at the time when the executive change took place the company was meeting new, tough competition, and far-reaching technological changes were in the making. The new president deemed it necessary to effect several changes in administrative personnel and to modify some of the long-standing policies of the company. Resentment was aroused in the complacent organization, and since all the members of the board of directors were department heads or other officials of the company, some of whose toes were being trodden upon, the new president did not receive their wholehearted backing and support.

[1] Copeland and Towl, *The Board of Directors and Business Management,* pp. 28–58.

After two years he resigned, and the retired ex-president came back. The former president could have provided a much more favorable environment for his successor by using his influence to have the board of directors reconstituted, with several well-chosen outside members, before the change took place. As it was, the cards were stacked against the new man from the start.

The functioning of a board of directors in the selection of a new chief executive is one of the most revealing tests of the competency of the board and of the retiring executive as an influential member of that board. The rubber-stamp type of board, for example, almost automatically approves whatever is recommended by the president of the company. Such a board approves a retirement program, if one is recommended by the boss, and accepts his candidate for a successor. On the other hand, if the boss chooses not to make any arrangements for retirement, the rubber-stamp board lets matters drift, probably until an emergency arises.

The type of executive who prefers to work with a rubber-stamp board and who succeeds in securing the election of such a board by the stockholders is especially likely to be reluctant to retire or to make any provision for retirement. Some of the saddest examples of companies which become ill and embarrassed are furnished by those which have been led, and led successfully for the time being, by strong, domineering executives with weak boards of directors. When the chief executive of such an enterprise passes away, often suddenly and perchance in time of crisis, frequently there is no successor in sight, and the machinery for promptly providing a new leader creaks and stalls. In such an instance the board of directors is not strong and alert enough to pick a competent successor promptly and to give him effective backing. The domineering executive has failed to do his part in facilitating the continued prosperous operation of the business. Such an executive also is not apt to have strong lieutenants among whom a competent successor may be found. A domineering executive is likely to have lieutenants who are "yes men" as well as to have directors who are rubber stamps. He is more of a dictator than a leader. Like a dictator, he can brook no rivals in power. And like a dictatorship his administrative structure tends to collapse when he no longer is there to run it.

It is in such situations, furthermore, that some of the most serious deficiencies in administrative housekeeping occur. When a board of directors is essentially a rubber-stamp outfit, the executive is left pretty much alone in his housekeeping, without effective inspection. The unclean spots eventually breed trouble, especially after that executive has passed away.

In contrast to these rubber-stamp situations are those in which a keen, able board of directors is alert to the problems of succession in management. The members of the board keep themselves informed regarding the policies of the company and the results attained. They observe the junior personnel and note prospective candidates for promotion. In other words the board inspects the administrative housekeeping and checks on the performance of the chief housekeepers. Thus an executive may facilitate the choice and induction of an able successor by using his influence toward the election of a board of directors which will be qualified to pick a competent successor to himself as well as to perform properly the other duties of a working board.

In order to facilitate further the work of a board of directors in choosing a new executive, an executive who is preparing to retire may provide a candidate for succession to his position. The nature of the problems that are involved in providing a candidate for succession can best be shown, it seems to me, by a few examples, especially in situations where provision for succession in management has been neglected.

One of these instances came to my attention several years ago in a case where the president of the company was eighty-five years old and the first vice president, who was slated to succeed him, was seventy-five years of age. The understanding that such a succession was to take place had been in effect for more than thirty years. If the president had retired at sixty or even at sixty-five, the vice president would not necessarily have been disqualified for the higher position on grounds of age. Under the circumstances, he constituted insurance for the emergency of a vacancy in the president's chair, but not for real succession in management. This is a very extreme case, of course, but it is a real one.

Here is another situation, of a much more common type. In 1938 the president of a large company died at the age of fifty-five. He had been ill a year earlier but seemed to have recovered. Then the end came suddenly. When the directors looked over the personnel of the organization, they found no one whom they deemed qualified to become president, and there was no reason for thinking that the situation would have been improved had the president continued in office for another ten years and then retired on schedule.

The senior vice president, who was in charge of production, was an able production man with an affable personality, but he had not had the all-round experience of topside management and he was close to the point of retirement. Incidentally but not unimportantly, his wife was *persona non grata* to the wives of some of the directors. Consequently he was not an acceptable candidate for the presidency.

The general sales manager, also a vice president, was about fifty years old. He was a genial individual with a great deal of energy and drive but given to snap judgments. He had a widespread acquaintance in the industry and the trade and was well liked. He prided himself on his analytical ability, but actually he was gullible for new schemes which sounded plausible, and once he had espoused a project he fought for it tenaciously with more or less disregard for weaknesses in the proposals and for objections which might be uncovered by others. He tended to surround himself, furthermore, with men who would rather blindly agree with him and support whatever position he took.

The treasurer of the company also was a personable man. He was about forty-five years old. He had a keen insight into the problems which arose within his jurisdiction, but he had an aversion to the making of major decisions. He sought to have someone else take that responsibility.

Each of these men had a fine character and certain estimable qualities, but each of them lacked the combination of qualities needed for leadership of the enterprise as a whole. In the lower ranks in the organization, furthermore, there was no individual of such outstanding ability that he could be vaulted over the senior officers into the presidency.

Under the circumstances the directors concluded that they must seek a man from outside to fill the position. It was several months before an acceptable candidate was found and after he took office an additional period of time was required for him to become acquainted with the personnel and with the details of the business. As a result the company lost momentum at a critical time. The loss of momentum was not disastrous but it was a handicap to the company in maintaining its position in a highly competitive industry.

The foregoing example arose out of an emergency caused by premature death. It shows, nevertheless, the need for preparation for succession. In other words preparation for retirement also can be preparation for emergencies.

One of the means by which an executive can aid in providing for succession in management is in the selection and development of his lieutenants. At this point we encounter two different theories on providing for succession.

One theory, often applied, is for the chief executive to select what he deems to be a promising lieutenant to be groomed as his successor. The candidate thus becomes a "crown prince." This procedure has the merit of a very definite provision for succession. It also may involve difficulties. When it becomes known within the organization that a particular individual has become the "crown prince," he is set apart from his previous peers, subject to both their criticism and their sycophancy, but without any real over-all authority. Sometimes the criticism and sycophancy directed toward a "crown prince" impair his ability eventually to establish his leadership. Furthermore, when the time comes for the directors to choose a new president, they may select someone other than the "crown prince." That happened in one company with whose affairs I was familiar, where an outsider was brought into the presidency and the prestige and effectiveness of the deposed "crown prince" were lessened both inside and outside the company.

In order to avoid possible misunderstanding, it may be well to point out again the distinction between having a "second-in-command" who may assume the duties of the chief executive in an emergency and a person who is being groomed as a permanent successor. In several companies the practice has developed of having a "second-in-command" who may be of approximately the same age as the chief executive and who participates in the consideration of top managerial problems and is thoroughly familiar with the top managerial duties. He usually has an assignment of particular duties and responsibilities, but it is expected that he can step in and run the top job in the event that the chief executive is incapacitated. That is insurance against temporary emergencies. A "crown prince," on the other hand, is a younger man, who may or may not be ready to step into the top job on short notice. He is looked upon as a leader in the next generation.

A contrasting procedure to that of setting up a "crown prince" is that of selecting and developing several lieutenants each of whom is hoped to have potential ability to handle the top executive job. During the period of development these lieutenants serve as department heads, and they are, in effect, put into competition with each other for the top job when a vacancy occurs.

A company in which there are several lieutenants, any one of whom has a genuine chance for winning the chief executive job, seems to me to be stronger than the company with a "crown prince." The former obviously has a greater reserve of executive manpower, and rivalry for the top job provides a strong incentive to each lieutenant to develop fully his executive abilities. After the selection of a new top executive finally has been made from among the lieutenants, when a vacancy does occur, some of the nonsuccessful rivals may be so disappointed, of course, that they will resign and go elsewhere. In my observation and experience such occasional losses are not too high a price to pay for the stimulus of competition for the job. It is likely to be better to have some turnover of high-grade men than to be staffed with mediocrities who cannot readily find new jobs elsewhere.

The conclusion to be drawn from these observations is that an executive best serves the interests of the enterprise of which he is the head, not by attempting to dictate the choice of his successor but by seeking to provide the administrative material from which a competent successor can be chosen when the occasion arises.

As has been pointed out above, the chief executive of a prosperous enterprise has a personal interest and pride in ensuring, if possible, the continued prosperity of the undertaking after his tenure ends. He will seek to have the good features of the old regime preserved and vital old policies continued. At the same time, if he really is wise, he will avoid placing a "dead hand" on the new leader. He will realize that his successor, if that man is competent, will uncover some weaknesses in the old regime which will need to be corrected and that practices and policies will have to be adapted to new conditions as changes arise.

As one who is about to retire, I can sympathize with a retiring executive who is apprehensive that soon after he is gone some of his pet schemes may be sacrificed, perhaps even in cold blood. As I view it, however, his task is not to try to prevent the sacrifice but rather to put himself in such a reconciled frame of mind that he can learn of the sacrifice without himself suffering acute pain therefrom and without raising any disturbance over it. Although a person has only one chance to practice it, graceful retirement is a real art.

For the good of the company

The purpose of having a definite retirement plan for executives is to promote the welfare of the company. While it is true that a board of directors has the authority to retire an executive whenever the board sees fit, it also is true in practice that in the absence of a definite retirement plan a board of directors frequently tends to permit an executive to hold his position even after his effectiveness has begun to wane. Most directors do not like to point their fingers at an executive with whom they have had long and pleasant associations and say, in effect: "Old man, you're slipping." When there is a fixed age for retirement, such finger-pointing is avoided.

If it were not for this reluctance of directors of business corporations and of corresponding boards of other types of institutions to stigmatize an aging executive, and if conclusive tests could be applied clearly to reveal decrepitude in its early stages, there would be much to be said in favor of judging each case by itself instead of having a fixed age for retirement. Some men begin to age, mentally as well as physically, in their early fifties. Others maintain their full vitality till they are seventy-five or perhaps eighty. Occasionally some old war horse possibly may be good until he is ninety. Yet, for the good of the company, it is better to risk losing the benefits of the contributions which a vigorous old executive could make than to suffer from an administration handicapped by decrepitude.

Sixty-five has become the customary age for the retirement of executives. Eventually when more experience has been accumulated and when keener scientific observations are possible, it may be found that sixty-five is not the right average age to use. At the present time, however, that retirement age is commonly deemed to give a company substantial protection against senility without sacrificing too much of the productive power of its senior executives. At all events, at this juncture I obviously am disqualified from venturing to express any opinion as to whether the retirement age for executives should be fixed at sixty-five or seventy or some other age.

One of the reasons often cited for having a retirement plan for executives is the stimulus which it furnishes younger men in the organization by affording them opportunities for promotion without too long a wait. Personally, I do not place great stock in that argument, and for two reasons. First, if it were true, it could be met by planning the age schedule of employees slated to be potential executive candidates so that they would be sufficiently younger than the top executives to be willing to wait for their chance. Secondly, in view of the scarcity of top executive talent, I cannot believe that even in the absence of retirement plans much competent executive material has been smothered by lack of opportunity for advancement. Perhaps those who expect that executive promotions will be made on a seniority basis may rely with confidence on this argument about bolstering morale; but for the good of the company, seniority should be a secondary consideration in the choice of a new top executive.

From the standpoint of providing for succession in management, however, there is a real advantage in having a regular, announced retirement plan. Not only can an executive then retire without losing face or feeling that he is being thrown into the discard, but under such a plan the date when a successor must be chosen, unless fate enters sooner, is definitely known and can be planned for. If there is no such program with a specified retirement age, provisions for replacement necessarily must involve a high degree of uncertainty. Will a successor be needed in two years or in twenty years? Such uncertainty is not conducive to the continual smooth functioning of a corporation.

While on this subject of retirement for the good of the company, I am going to take the liberty of adding a few observations regarding the retirement of directors. I have found that the retirement of directors is a subject with which some of the men in several companies are greatly concerned. Since our book on directors was published, Mr. Towl and I have had a number of inquiries on this subject, some of them urgent, including a couple of long-distance telephone calls from Chicago. The problem appears to be a particularly troublesome one in certain companies where there has been practically no turnover in the boards for a period of years. In such a case, as a result of low turnover, the board has become clogged with superannuated members who contribute little themselves and who occupy places which could be filled with energetic men, mentally alert, and able to come to grips with new problems. In some instances, furthermore, a board of this sort fails to make adequate provision for the retirement of executives. When the members of a board are themselves reluctant to retire, they are rather prone to dodge plans for executive retirement.

When a man has served on a board of directors for a long period of time, with only infrequent changes in the membership of the board, he well may be reluctant to break the association and to step out. Because of long and friendly association with him, his fellow members are hesitant about using their influence to push him out. Hence he stays on.

For dealing with this problem of securing the retirement of decrepit directors with as little pain as possible, there are at least three courses open. One is to have a fixed age limit set by vote of the stockholders. A second is to adopt a plan of rotation, whereby no director may serve continuously for more than three or five years. In a number of companies, in order to assure continuity of policies, the directors are elected for three- or five-year terms, with one-third or one-fifth of the board being elected each year, instead of having all the members elected for one-year terms. But, so far as I am aware, in none of those cases is there any rule against the reëlection of a member whose term has expired. Any such rule against reelection might deprive the company of the services of some of its abler directors of mature middle age or at least break the continuity of their services, and continuity of service is highly important in such a policy-making board. Such a forced rotation would be a high price to pay for getting rid of an occasional superannuated director.

The third possibility is to stimulate a greater turnover in the board on an informal schedule, so that no stigma of decrepitude will attach to the dropping of any one member. While this third plan has a good deal of merit, my rather tentative expectation is that eventually it will become common practice to have a fixed age for the retirement of directors as well as for the retirement of executives. That appears to be the surest and least painful solution.

For executives a retirement plan always includes, so far as I am aware, a provision for pensions. Such a provision is expected to provide reasonable assurance to the individual of an economic competence when he gives up his salary. Thus a pension system removes one of the obstacles to retirement, although as I have pointed out it may not be by any means the greatest obstacle.

During the last ten years, when income taxes have been so high, there has been a strong tendency for executive pensions to be substantially increased. Typically these pensions represent deferred executive compensation. If an executive receives a salary of $50,000 a year and assurance of a pension of $25,000 a year after retirement, he is substantially better off taxwise than if he were to receive a salary currently of $75,000 a year.

I shall not go into this subject of pensions at length because it has been treated comprehensively by others.[2] There are a few observations of my own, however, which I wish to make for what they may be worth.

On the subject of pensions in general, I cannot refrain from pointing out that to some extent they are one of the mirages of security. For many years a certain amount has been deducted from my pay check each month to provide a pension for me on retirement. Many of my dollars which were deducted are now worth not over one third of what they were worth at the time of deduction. I have no complaint to make, but it obviously is true that a large number of pensioners have been victimized by the devaluation of the dollar and its sub-

[2] On the subject of the effects of federal income taxes on executive behavior and on pension plans, the results of two research studies were published in 1951 by the Division of Research, Harvard Business School. One study is by Professor Thomas H. Sanders and the other by Professor Challis A. Hall, Jr.

sequent depreciation. They have not received the security for which they paid.

So far as the pensions of business executives are concerned, unless they are vested their payment customarily is dependent upon the continued profitable operation of the companies by which they are employed. If we run into a period of hard times again, as we almost certainly shall, some of those companies are likely to have difficulty in meeting all their obligations, including pledges for executive pensions. Other changes in the business environment sooner or later, it seems to me, also are bound to jeopardize some of the executive pension commitments. In making these statements it is not at all my purpose to condemn pension plans. I merely am aiming to point out that these plans may produce some mirages of security in this ever changing world.

Another and far more serious problem pertaining to executive pensions is latent in those companies which look upon executive pensions as deferred compensation rather than as reserves for retirement to be built up on the same principle as is applied to the building of pensions for other employees. Executives may be able to rationalize grounds on which their scale of pensions should be governed by principles different from those which govern the pensions of other employees. It appears to me, however, to be extremely unlikely that they can secure acceptance of their rationalizations by the rank and file of the employees or by the public at large.

Only a few days ago a lady professor at another institution remarked: "How is it possible for the executives of some of these companies to make provision for such huge pensions as they are to receive?" She assumed that the pensions of business executives were based on the same contributory principles as apply to teachers' pensions. I am sure that her attitude toward liberal compensation for business executives of the companies in which she is a small stockholder is far more sympathetic than that of many men on the street and in the factories, but she has great difficulty in grasping the basis for rationalizing different standards of pension treatment for business executives. Whatever the merits of their case, I doubt whether business executives ever will succeed in securing general acceptance of a basis for pension treatment essentially different from that which applies to other employees.

As I have tried to indicate, this subject of pensions and retirement is one which is fraught with great emotions, and anything which might be interpreted as discrimination in the plans or in the administration of the plans for retirement adds fuel to the emotional flames. Whether the following anecdote is true, I do not know. But the zest with which it has been circulated in Cambridge during the last twenty years has given an indication of some of the emotion attaching to retirement. When a certain professor reached the regular retiring age, so the story goes, he received the customary notice from the president of the university, whereupon the professor wrote the following note to the president: "Sir I, Professor N. W. ———, aged 65, about to be retired, salute President A. Lawrence Lowell, aged 75."

Personal outlook

As I have stated earlier, this subject of retirement is one of immediate concern to me personally. I was ready to retire and now, in the view of some of my friends at least, I have been granted a reprieve. Consequently I have a somewhat intimate acquaintance with an approach to retirement.

For my part, I am looking forward to retirement with pleasant anticipations. Among other things, I expect to enjoy a second boyhood, and I am somewhat impatient because the deferring of my retirement is interfering with a realization of those expectations.

One of the first questions to arise as a person approaches

retirement is where to live. We have solved that problem very happily. In fact a proposal to change our living quarters was what first brought me face to face with the problem of retirement. For many years we had lived in Cambridge, with a summer home in a cottage on the Annisquam River in Gloucester, Massachusetts. Mrs. Copeland, however, was finding the responsibility of two houses rather burdensome, and from time to time we had discussed casually having one year-round home. Then late in the fall of 1943, when I was fifty-nine years old, we spent a week end with friends at their summer home in Annisquam, about a mile and a half from our own cottage. It was a delightful, clear, sparkling, invigorating week end, and shortly thereafter Mrs. Copeland and I decided to start looking for a place in that neighborhood to buy for a year-round residence. That meant, in effect, that we would plan to live there after I had retired.

Until then I had given only a few casual thoughts to retirement. I was busy with my work, and I was prone not to try to cross distant bridges until I reached them. It never had occurred to me, furthermore, that there was such a thing as "retirement shock." And as yet I have experienced no such shock myself.

Two years after having decided to try to find a new year-round home, we bought a place in Annisquam, a delightful little, old-fashioned village on Ipswich Bay. Later we remodeled and fully winterized the house, cleared the brush off some of the ill-kept land, and began a rather extensive landscaping job, which is not wholly finished. We sold our Cambridge house and are now well settled in our new home.

We have an acre and a half of land and ledge, the lot being quite irregular in shape. It is situated on the top of a hill. From the chair in my study where I am now writing I look out to the westward over the lawn and rocks, through a long corridor of trees and ledges, at the waters of Ipswich Bay, the sandy beaches in West Gloucester and Essex where on occasion striped bass are caught, the marshes bordering the Essex River, and the distant hills of Ipswich, Rowley, and Topsfield.

By changing my position, I look through another window to the southward over the treetops at the winding Annisquam River, which is not really a river but a tidal stream connecting Gloucester harbor with Ipswich Bay and thereby making Cape Ann an island. In the distance, up the river, I can see our former cottage, where we spent twenty-three happy summers. Consequently the surroundings are familiar ones, a fact which may have real significance when it comes to retirement. Like many other men, I am especially fond of old shoes and old clothes, old friends, and familiar scenes.

To the eastward, through still another window I look across the roofs and the trees in the village to the moors of deserted Dogtown Common beyond Lobster Cove and Goose Cove. From blueberrying excursions I have gained some familiarity with Dogtown, but for me that is still one of the intriguing areas for exploration. To the northward we are sheltered by hill and rocks and trees and houses from the wintry blasts of the north and northwest winds.

For us this is a highly satisfactory place in which to retire. This brief description almost answers the question as to what I shall do to keep time from hanging heavy on my hands. First in order of pressure, if not of interest, is the care of the grounds. There are always shrubs to be trimmed or moved, trees to be trimmed or cut down and sawed up for firewood, crabgrass and weeds in the lawn to be killed, and dozens of other chores. I could spend all my time on such work, but I shall not do so.

For five or six months in the year there are fishing opportunities to be given a high priority on my time schedule. At this very moment this writing is interfering with my fishing — at this season of the year for striped bass or mackerel. Although this last summer was a wretched one from the fishing standpoint, ordinarily for a period of nearly three months the tuna fishing in Ipswich Bay is one of the most exciting sports to be found anywhere, the fish taken on rod and reel usually ranging from 100 to 900 pounds each in weight, with 300- to 500-pounders being most common. I still hope to catch a few more of them. An occasional shark adds annoyance, if not excitement, to the tuna fishing.

Then there are other possibilities. About a mile off the eastern end of the Cape is a ledge where I fished once successfully for tautog some years ago. I haven't yet found time to go back, but I envisage a lot of potential fun there. So far as I am aware I am the only person interested in that spot. Then there is a deep hole off Turks Head where I once hooked onto a fish that broke my line. That particular fish probably has gone into fish cakes or suffered some worse fate. Nevertheless it is a locality which warrants reëxamination. These are only a few of the possibilities awaiting attention.

Then, if I have an intellectual urge once in a while, I have plenty of pencils and paper for writing. And there are numerous other activities of various types to which I am already committed which will place demands on some of my time. I am already apprehensive, furthermore, that some new and unforeseen demand will interfere with the plans that I tentatively have in mind for utilizing my leisure.

Then there's the reading to which I also have been looking forward these many years — adventure stories and the like, old and new — books which I could not afford to buy when I was a youngster and which I could not afford the time to read when I was sufficiently affluent to buy an occasional pleasure book. As a boy I was an avid reader of such literature, when I could get access to it, and I still have a hankering for it.

Obviously one's outlook on retirement depends very much

upon the individual's outlook on life. To some, retirement is going down the other side of the hill. Personally I prefer to look at the sunsets.

As I cast my eyes out across the bay in the evening the sunset frequently is very beautiful, with bright and rapidly changing colors of fleecy clouds. Sometimes the sun sets in a clear, cloudless sky, with no striking aftereffects. Or it may set in a mellow haze, betokening a balmy day to come. Sometimes the bay is covered with a thick fog, but the fogs usually come in the morning rather than the evening. On still other evenings, without fog, the sky is dark and cloudy, over a gray, grim, relentless sea. But we always know that above the dark clouds the sun is setting brightly and that presently we shall have some more stimulating and lovely sunsets.

Sunsets may be mirages, and I may be getting ready to whistle in the dark. But so far I have felt no queasiness at the thought of retiring. As to my preparation for retirement, it would not be far from the truth, I believe, to say that for the last sixty years I have been getting ready to retire.

XIV

Freedom for Achievement

Here in America business executives still have opportunity to exercise initiative and leadership. In various other quarters of the world, however, business management is being superseded by political management of industry, and that political management, like an octopus, is ever reaching out its tentacles to clasp more enterprises into its maw. The greatest political octopus at the present time, of course, is in Russia, but Russia is by no means the only country in which political octopuses are spawning, nor are they always a detectable red in color.

Political management of industry

Communism of the Russian brand seems to constitute the greatest threat to our freedom at the present time. If we are not annihilated by the Red fanatics of the Kremlin in the near future, however, the creeping forms of socialism actually are more dangerous. The insidious manner in which the less extreme forms of socialism tend slowly to draw people within their clasp may allay resistance until it is too late to resist successfully.

The ultimate aim of the socialists avowedly is government ownership of the means of production, that is of all industry, in order to eliminate private gain from interest and profits.

Government ownership, however, means political administration, and it is the administrative aspects of the socialist state with which we should be particularly concerned.

In all the controversy over Marxian socialism during the last century, it is noteworthy that practically no attention, so far as I am aware, has been given to the administrative problems of a socialist state. It is not to be wondered that Karl Marx and his disciples did not comprehend or take any interest in administration. Their theory was developed far from any administrative responsibility, and it was of a mechanistic sort. The critics of socialism also generally have directed their comments toward that mechanistic theory, apparently without recognizing its limited significance. Both the socialists and their critics generally have devoted their attention to the ownership of the means of production and the returns gained therefrom rather than to the problems of managing the enterprises where the tools of production are used.

Those problems of administration are complicated, rather than simplified, by a socialization of industry. Even in a socialist state machines cannot manage themselves. And unless individual tastes are eliminated, the products of the machines cannot be distributed pro rata to every consumer; marketing too must be managed even in a socialist state.

Government administration tends notoriously to be bureaucratic. In the administrative agencies decisions usually are made slowly and so far as possible "safely." The typical bureaucrat takes his time, in order to be "safe," and then tries to avoid making any decision which might boomerang on him. "Passing the buck" is popularly known as "the old army game," but it is a game typical of bureaucratic administration. Under political management the bureaucrats inevitably tend to build up an elaborate set of rules for self-protection. Government rules and regulations — "red tape" — furnish convenient alibis for inaction. So long as the rules are observed a man may expect to hold his job. That attitude stifles experiment, innovation, and change. For a government official to make an unsuccessful experiment, with potential political investigators lurking in the background, is a far more serious risk than to do nothing.

The head of a government undertaking, furthermore, is likely to have less freedom in the hiring and firing of his lieutenants than is the case in a private enterprise; political pressure for preferential treatment of recommended individuals oftentimes cannot be completely withstood.

The reliance on rules for alibis, the pressure for accepting political appointments, and the diffused responsibility for government policies quite generally dull initiative in political management. There are still many shortcomings, to be sure, in the executive management of private enterprises, but generally there is far better opportunity at present for correcting those deficiencies in private enterprise than for overcoming the dulling influences in political management.

Socialism substitutes bureaucracy for independent executive judgment and action and thus has a stifling effect on administration. The costs of bureaucratic administration, furthermore, are likely to far outweigh the savings anticipated by the elimination of private profits. The "overhead" of a socialist state, except perhaps under a dictatorship, will cost consumers through taxes or indirect levies more than can be saved in "interest" and profits.

In a socialist regime political and economic power is in the hands of the same group. The administration of production, distribution, finance, and all the other activities which in America we call "business" are under the supervision of political bosses. The heads of the operating bureaus are lieutenants of the politicians, and the deputy administrators or commissars carry out their orders. The concentration of political power and industrial administration in the hands of the same group of officials is one of the main reasons why socialism is likely to end up in dictatorship.

The irony of the situation here in America at present is that so many people will agree fully that socialism is dangerous and that communism is terrible but at the same time will support individual proposals for socialization which really are subtle steps toward the establishment of a socialized state.

This subject of socialism and the political management of industry is so provocative that there is a temptation to ramble on in an almost endless discussion of its ramifying implications and of the numerous factors which have caused it to spread. I will content myself, however, with raising only one more question: Would it be possible for socialism and communism to avoid stagnation within a fairly short period of time if there were no other country in which the leaven of private enterprise were continually setting new goals for emulation?

Opportunities for achievement

A really healthy society is one in which there are opportunities for leaders to emerge from all ranks in the population. For biological and other causes which as yet are little understood, the genius of leadership seems as likely to sprout in some humble cottage as in a mansion of the well-to-do. Early schooling in humble surroundings where little luxury is enjoyed and where perhaps even hardship must be experienced is not a handicap to the attainment of leadership. Those of us who have gone through such a schooling rather naturally desire that our children and grandchildren should not have to encounter the same sort of a struggle. Yet by sheltering them from that type of experience, it seems that sometimes we render them a disservice.

In my boyhood days the Horatio Alger stories of ragged

boys who attained success were highly popular. To the present generation of sophisticated youngsters the Alger boys are unknown, and I am not informed as to whether anyone comparable has taken their place. Be that as it may, I judge that beneath their veneer of sophistication the younger generation of Americans still harbor a good deal of that same spirit of ambition. At all events that is some of the stuff of which leaders are made.

Where there are opportunities for leaders to emerge from every segment of the population, the broadest base exists for the development of qualities essential to a high level of executive achievement. The qualities essential for leadership are by no means universally transmitted from father to son. Decadent princes of royal stock and "playboy" and shirt-sleeve offspring of successful business executives obviously are not uncommon. Hence the importance of having a healthy crop of competent leadership candidates available from other sources. Thus freedom from barriers of social caste and freedom from autocratic or bureaucratic political restraints on opportunities for advancement contribute to the supplying of able men for positions of constructive administration.

In the business field freedom of the market place, freedom for starting new enterprises, and freedom of investment also are essential if full opportunity is to be afforded for the development of vigorous enterprises.

Freedom of the market place means freedom of consumers to bestow their patronage where they choose and freedom of producers and merchants to compete for consumers' patronage. Where such freedom exists, consumers ultimately determine by their purchases what enterprises are to have an opportunity to prosper. In a free market place, however, manufacturers and merchants are not merely the passive recipients of consumer patronage. They can seek to influence the actions of consumers by price adjustments, by modifications and improvements in products, by services offered, and by the various means of sales promotion with which we are all so familiar. Thus a free market place affords opportunity for the exercise of ingenuity and resourcefulness. Such conditions are especially conducive to executive achievement.

Under freedom of the market place, the government merely sets up certain safeguards against fraud or misrepresentation, such as are embodied in the Pure Food and Drugs Act and similar legislation, and seeks to assure freedom of purchase and sale. So long as there is no misrepresentation or coercion, the consumer decides how he wants to spend his income, rather than have some more or less well-meaning bureaucrat decide it for him. This freedom to cater to consumers' desires and to stimulate latent wants places a premium on energetic and resourceful business management.

The alternative to freedom of the market place is regimentation, whereby political managers determine more or less arbitrarily what consumers may be permitted to procure. When they are free to buy what they choose, consumers sometimes may be whimsical or impulsive or even gullible. But such shortcomings are less disadvantageous than the stagnating influence of political management of industry.

Freedom of the market place also facilitates the starting of new enterprises. During recent years many efforts have been made in this country to protect and foster "small business," efforts with which in general I am heartily in accord. Nevertheless, "small business" is a rather nondescript term, since a small business in the retail grocery trade or in the garment industry, for example, is not at all comparable to a small business in the electrical or chemical manufacturing industries. The dynamic small business is the growing enterprise.[1] It is to new growing enterprises that we must look for the maintenance of full employment and for the preservation of a healthy economy. As consumers' tastes shift and as other factors cause some of the established concerns to falter and fail, it is of vital importance that their places be taken by new enterprises and that there be no road blocks against the starting of new ventures.

There is a widespread opinion nowadays that it is difficult if not impossible for a new enterprise to get started in the face of the competition from big, established companies. As a generalization that view is false. While economies of large-scale operation are such in the automobile industry, for example, that a new company must start on a big scale, with ample financial resources, if it is to have any chance for success, nevertheless small-scale newcomers are continually finding opportunities for the manufacture of accessories and parts for the automobile trade. In other industries, such as electrical and chemical manufacturing, and book publishing, relatively small companies are operating successfully alongside the large corporations. Typically in such industries the small company concentrates on the manufacture and marketing of specialized items with which the large companies cannot afford to bother or in the handling of which they are commercially clumsy. As I have pointed out in an earlier chapter, the small company often has a flexibility and a maneuverability which the large company does not match. There are many interstices in industry where the resourceful, energetic small operator can get a foothold and grow. If he has the ingenuity to devise a product or service which consumers potentially want and if he has the resourcefulness and

[1] The following research studies, published by the Harvard Business School, deal with some of the problems of growing enterprises: J. Keith Butters and John Lintner, *Effect of Federal Taxes on Growing Enterprises* (1945), and Paul F. Lawler, *Records for the Control of Growing Manufacturing Enterprises* (1947).

administrative ability to put it on the market, even in a modest way, he can make a start. Examples to prove this point readily can be noted, ranging all the way from diaper service to helicopters.

Some new ventures will fail. That is bound to be true so long as we have freedom of enterprise. Some men who start new undertakings will not have managerial "know-how" or the ability to acquire it. They must be permitted to fail. Freedom implies risk-taking and when risks are taken there inevitably will be some losers. In one sense this is one method of trying out candidates for executive undertakings and of weeding out those who prove not to have the ability to carry the ball.

Those who fail will have alibis, of course, for their non-success. Many an amateur inventor, for example, fails to put his inventions successfully into production and sale and eventually blames the "pirates" who take over and make a success of the enterprise. It seems to be rather characteristic of such inventors that they have little knack of management and no real respect for those who can turn crude inventions into commercial successes. The socialists are by no means the only people who have no appreciation of administrative problems and of administrative ability.

Despite some failures in these new ventures, enough have survived and are surviving to encourage more to be undertaken. The experience of starting a new enterprise frequently is tough, but from among those promoters who come through that experience successfully emerge some of our most competent executives. Under a bureaucracy, furthermore, there is no such freedom in taking the risk of starting new ventures and so far as I can see no other gains which offset that loss.

Closely related to freedom of the market place and freedom to start new enterprises is freedom of investment. Freedom to invest, subject to police protection against misrepresentation and fraud, is essential to enable enterprises to obtain funds with which to compete for consumers' patronage. Freedom to invest also means freedom to take risks and to incur loss when mistakes in judgment occur.

The alternative to freedom of investment is forced savings by means of taxation or some similar device. The control of capital investments by a bureaucracy determines what enterprises can be carried on and what cannot be undertaken. The judgment of the bureaucrats is substituted for the operation of the market place. And, of course, the judgment of the bureaucrats hardly will be free from the influence of politicians who usually are intent on winning votes in order to perpetuate their influence. From such controls the sinews of dictatorship are derived.

Freedom of the market place, freedom for starting new enterprises, and freedom of investment facilitate the attainment of a higher standard of living for the community and of improved social conditions. They encourage experiment, innovation, and improvement in technological methods and administrative procedures and thereby stimulate economic and social progress.

A few conclusions

The attainment of authority by securing the voluntary acceptance of leadership is essentially a democratic process. The methods of communication between employees and management in order to facilitate a true acceptance of leadership are not yet perfectly developed in most American industries, but progress is constantly being made toward that end. And the attention now being given in many companies to the attaining of a better understanding of human relations in industry is one of the main features of that progress. These efforts basically recognize the self-respect and the dignity of the individual employee as a human being whatever his place in the whole undertaking may be. The voluntary development of effective teamwork within each enterprise is a mark of genuine executive achievement. That is the antithesis of totalitarian management of industry.

The choosing of lieutenants who can function voluntarily and wholeheartedly as members of an administrative team and who in turn can secure acceptance of their leadership within their respective spheres is likewise an inherent characteristic of freedom for executive achievement. And the development of lieutenants, especially through coaching, to become broad-gauge administrators is another democratic process.

Freedom for economic achievement is a privilege. In the business field it is a privilege to aid in the organizing and guidance of productive enterprises and useful services which the users patronize of their own free will. It affords opportunities for enlisting and retaining the loyalty and support of employees and investors, distributors and consumers in the conduct of mutually advantageous undertakings.

Freedom for executive achievement connotes the privilege of starting new enterprises, even at the risk of loss, as well as of aspiring to reach the top in established concerns. It also connotes the privilege of plunging into the vortex of ever-changing conditions with no definite assurance of survival. It means the taking of risks of financial loss, of jeopardy to health, even of sacrifice of personal reputation. Among the rewards for those who successfully survive those risks, the personal satisfaction of being of service to the community is by no means the least. Out of these risky ventures come some of the greatest contributions to the comfort and welfare of mankind.

Freedom for executive achievement, therefore, is essentially the opportunity for a competent executive to serve as a catalytic agent in accelerating the reaction of all those who are associated with him in the enterprise to render a service which their patrons will support and which will contribute to human welfare. With such freedom in the past great progress has been made. With such freedom in the future there is opportunity for still greater progress to be achieved.

INDEX

Index

Bei Fragen zur Produktsicherheit wenden Sie sich bitte an:
If you have any questions regarding product safety,
please contact:

Walter de Gruyter GmbH
Genthiner Straße 13
10785 Berlin
productsafety@degruyterbrill.com